CLOSING THE TRUST GAP

TAKING ACTION ON WHAT MATTERS MOST FOR LEADERS, TEAMS, AND ORGANIZATIONS

CORY SCHEER, ED.D.

Closing the Trust Gap
Taking Action on What Matters Most for Leaders, Teams, and Organizations

Published by Streamline Books
www.streamlinebookspublishing.com

Book Cover Design by Hannah Crabb

ISBN:
979-8-89165-047-3 *Paperback*
979-8-89165-048-0 *Hardback*
979-8-89165-049-7 *E-book*

For Jamie, Cailyn, Isaac, Evan, and Levi:

I love you with everything.

CONTENTS

FOREWORD

BY JUSTIN RICKLEFS

When trust is broken, all seems lost.

Especially when you're the one doing the breaking.

In 2016, my dad had open-heart surgery, and as I sat in the waiting room, my wife kept texting me.

"We need to talk."

Didn't she know I was needed in that helpless waiting room? I stepped into the terribly lit corridor and called her. My world was crumbling, and I knew it. Or more specifically, trust was crumbling.

The details are irrelevant. What is relevant, though, is that I was living my life in a way that eroded the very ingredient necessary for a flourishing partnership:

Trust.

Over the past seven years, I've been on a journey. A journey of doing the specific, helpful, and good (but definitely not easy) work of closing the trust gaps I've created. In that same period of time, I've been building a business—a business born in the midst of my own undoing. A business that cares about the culture of its people. A business that cares deeply about the experience of its clients. A business that has benefited from the journey of the darker nights of my soul. And, most certainly, a business that is better because of my friendship with Cory Scheer and the work he's doing to help organizations and their leaders close the gap between distrust and truth. He helps move them from toxic to trustworthy.

At Guild Collective, Cory's fingerprints—and his heart—have been all over what we've created. Before we even launched publicly, Cory and I sat down on our screened-in porch, and he helped me architect what became our first content delivery system. As our team grew, the business became more beautiful and complicated. So, we've brought Cory into the most intimate of places in our story: into our boardroom, with our clients, with our team, and on stage sharing to the collective of humans we're trying to ignite and inspire—humans who are brave enough to share their hearts.

His work is woven into the fabric of our performance review process (we call them "Pathways"), our team member insight process (we call them "Perspectives"), our onboarding practices, and in the casual coffee conversations. Trust is even a core value written into the ethos of our company. Put simply, our business is stronger. The culture of our team and the experience of our clients is greater because we have let this good work saturate into our souls, systems, and structure.

The Trust Proposition that helps close the trust gap is far from theoretical. It's the most practical tool we've found.

If you hang around owners, leaders, and marketers long enough, you're bound to hear talk about value propositions, positioning statements, and some other jargon that makes you feel less smart and less human. But with Cory, the simple and strategic framework he shares allows leaders to cut through the nonsense and see how human behavior impacts (and impedes) the good work we each are made to do.

Long before you can create value, or build loyalty in an organization, there must be a foundation built on trust. Without it, we have no shot. With it, we can move mountains.

Cory's work, and his reflections in this book, are worth your soul's weight in gold. If you're a leader who cares about your own impact, the health of your team, and the experience of your clients, this timeless and transformational treasure is for you.

When the trust gap is closed, life gets better.

Trust me. I've lived it.

Justin Ricklefs
Founder and CEO
Guild Collective

FOREWORD

INTRODUCTION

At the heart of every organization lies a silent crisis: the erosion of trust.

Through the countless conversations I have had with leaders, teams, and organizations over the years, one consistent, troubling insight emerged: a staggering trust deficit between employees and their leaders. These individuals readily share specific, vivid examples of the scars left by organizational distrust—weakened or ruined relationships, halted progress, and unsettling work culture dynamics. More than that, they often describe the tangible toll it takes—physical fatigue, emotional strain, and psychological distress.

No matter their level of leadership or the industry in which they work, most people share a collective, honest desire to be a part of an organization with a high level of intrinsic trust. They dream of a place free of destructive drama, where productivity and progress soar under the banner of genuine positivity.

But while they can imagine that high-trust environment, the path to get there remains illusive. They grapple with defining a genuine, proven framework, a guiding compass to guide their entire organization towards a thriving culture that embraces trust.

This chasm between present circumstances and a desirable future—the trust gap—is vast, troubling, and ever-widening. It's a gap that shakes people, makes them restless, and for some, brings them to tears.

And rightly so.

There's no question as to *why* trust is important. The challenge is being clear on *how* to tactically build trust with a proven and memorable framework that can be shared easily throughout an organization. In the absence of a common approach to close the trust gap, the priority of intentionally strengthening trust is often relegated to the personality and philosophy of the people who have the highest level of authority in decision-making. However, if the leaders are perceived as untrustworthy—a problem our research shows is pervasive—very little progress will be made to move the needle and improve the organization's culture.

In the busyness of all that occurs within an organization, the tyranny of urgency or the impact of a toxic team member can derail and de-prioritize trust. And if the strategy to strengthen trust is "Priority #4"—that is, always on the list but never getting done, or only discussed as something philosophical instead of practical—trust will stay unattainable and invisible.

A trustless work culture is fueled by lazy efforts to be clear and committed to strengthening trust. In a one hundred-person company, if one hundred employees each have their own version of what trust is and their own reasons why they should or shouldn't take action to strengthen it, the overall commitment to building organizational trust will be diluted, fractured, confusing, and ultimately ineffective. This not only affects team members who are part of the workplace culture, but also the people the organization is attempting to serve, retain, and invite into promoting their products and services to others.

When it comes to the question of *how* to build and strengthen trust, everyone in the organization needs to be clear. Thankfully it can be clear, because if it weren't clear there would be no hope for the future of the health and well-being of the organizational culture. There would be no long-lasting reason for an employee to stay. Every employee in every organization needs (and deserves) to be equipped with a simple, memorable and actionable framework that helps them strengthen relational and organizational trust.

It's impossible to argue *against* the benefits of trust. I've yet to meet a person that has told me that trust is "not really that important." I've yet to hear of an "anti-trust strengthening" movement. Yet more and more organizations behave in a way that widens the trust gap. The research on the ever-widening trust gap within small, medium, and large companies alike is staggering.

For example, a recent survey from PwC "showed a large trust gap that is not budging—because while everyone agrees trust is important, people seem to have different definitions of what makes or breaks trust and that 54% of employees report experiencing a trust-damaging event, compared to only 20% of executives."[1]

Elements Global Services, an HR technology company also found that "76% of workers who use a computer are concerned about their employer monitoring their communications and 74% of those who work remotely are concerned about their employer monitoring when and how much they work."[2]

And Gallup has found that only 21% of American workers "strongly agree" that they trust the leaders of their organization, which is down from 24% in 2019.[3] Worse, Gallup also found that over half of employees are actively or passively job-seeking, and that "when combined with actively disengaged employees, low engagement costs the global economy $8.8 trillion dollars, or 9% of global GDP."[4]

In other words? People everywhere, in every industry, at every level are experiencing the detrimental impact of the trust gap. The economy itself suffers for it.

Leaders who choose to wait for trust to magically appear or rely on trite, cliché efforts to improve morale (i.e. pizza party Fridays, employee of the month awards, email-only encouragement) will be sorely disappointed to see that their organization's culture is eroding.

The current and very troubling condition of trust is a clarion call to action. Despite the dismal data showing pervasive organizational distrust, every organization has the opportunity to assess their current level of trust, learn, and then adopt a proven framework for strengthening trust. They have the opportunity to commit to developing a plan to close the trust gap.

Closing the Trust Gap is designed to bring hope and impact to those professionals who find themselves in a new season or chapter of influence, regardless of title. Maybe you are brand new to leading people, and up until this point, you've never been responsible for the outcomes of a team. Or, maybe you're an aspiring leader taking formal steps to gain more oversight and responsibility. Because the newness of your influence or leadership role is still fresh, the challenges of wrapping your mind around the dynamics of the workplace culture are probably very real.

Even seasoned leaders benefit from learning how meetings are best facilitated, how decisions are made versus how they should be made, how the challenges of the past are still showing up in the present, how policies and practices inform day-to-day activities, the nuances of edgy emails (or emails that are never replied to), and how to navigate the awkwardness of conversations that are occurring in hallways, parking lots, and private Slack channels.

And if you are a seasoned leader, you are still subject to finding yourself in a role where the dynamics are different from what you have experienced in past organizations. It could be that you have been in the same managerial role for some time, but the organization or team you are leading is changing, growing, pivoting, struggling, or wandering from its mission. It isn't uncommon to feel ongoing frustration due to a lack of clarity on how to best proceed. Or, you may be sensing something that doesn't feel right. Your trust radar is consistently flashing yellow and red lights, but you are struggling to articulate, assess, and take action on improving these distrust dynamics.

Regardless of the season of work a person finds themselves in, one of the realities of low-trust organizations is that, if left unaddressed, low-burn frustration turns into a troubling employee realization: that they're not going to last in this organization.

Why?

Because they don't trust it.

Once a person has come to this conclusion, an internal timer starts ticking. From there, it's no longer a matter of *if*, but *when* the employee will be leaving this organization behind. Worse, they feel they have no reason to look back. Thus, the all too common resignation wheel continues to turn, and high turnover becomes "just the way it is."

Confusion turns into frustration. Frustration turns into apathy. Apathy turns into a sense of hopelessness that nothing can be done. As a result, the trust gap gets wider. This tragic, *avoidable* outcome is the reason why I'm so passionate about helping leaders, teams, and organizations take action on strengthening trust. Regardless of what season of influence you, your employees, or your own leaders are in, the need for strengthening trust is great, and the time to take action is now.

Practically speaking, there are powerful benefits to strengthening trust in your workplace:

- Your staff retention will increase. There will be less employee turnover, saving your organization time and money.
- Your workplace will become less toxic.
- Your employees will work harder, and cynicism will be replaced with creative and collaborative work.
- Advocacy from your employees to recruit other team members to work for your organization will also increase.
- Outdated policies rooted in the status quo can be evaluated accurately once and for all so that your organization can move forward.
- You'll be able to close the gap between leaders, middle managers, and front-line employees.
- Your team will have clearer communication, more honest conversations, and more opportunities to establish and carry out agreed-upon expectations.
- Your team will have more resilience as you move forward through conflict and change management.
- Ultimately, by building and strengthening trust, you'll improve the crucial KPIs that will make your organization more successful.

There is hope. You can close the trust gap with your coworkers, your teams, and your organization.

Trust is a human value, and it exists in every relationship. Trust is the fuel for the engine of positive relationships and productive teams. Trust is a universal truth that is foundational for culture at large, as well as every organization.

Yet trust, despite its inarguable benefits and infinite potential, is often illusive, and organizations commonly behave in a way that suggests trust is not achievable.

This book has the power to help you transform trust from something intangible to something tactical, tangible, and even transformational. *Closing the The Trust Gap* is designed to provide you with a clear understanding of the chasms in trust that currently plague all industries and have significant implications for the work you do, the teams you lead or are a part of, and the organizations in which you serve. This framework, originally developed by a team of researchers in the early 2000s, is applicable now more than ever.[5]

It's one thing to talk about trust. It's something entirely different to have the courage to identify gaps and strengthen that trust. Join me as we roll up our sleeves, take action, and start closing the trust gap.

Trust is the firm belief in the truth of something.

CHAPTER 1
THE TRUST GAP

Recently my wife, Jamie, ordered an iced tea from a local fast-food restaurant. Nothing seemed out of the ordinary during the initial drive-thru ordering process: we waited in a long drive-through line moving at a glacial pace and enjoyed our patience being thoroughly tested. We spoke extra loudly into a wall-sized menu. We repeated our order with more volume when it wasn't heard the first time, inched forward, and waited some more.

Finally, the small double door windows snapped open. Greasy goodness was only moments away.

But as the fast food employee opened the window and passed Jamie her drink, Jamie noticed something was wrong. The iced tea was in a small cup, even though Jamie had ordered a large (we have four kids—maximum caffeine is a must).

No problem. Jamie politely told the worker that she had ordered a larger size and handed the cup back to him.

The employee took the cup from her without saying a word, and he disappeared back into the building as the windows slammed shut behind him. A minute later, the windows swung back open, and he handed her the iced tea. Without missing a beat, and without any emotion, he looked at Jamie and informed her:

"They don't pay me enough to care."

The window doors snapped shut again, and we slowly rolled away in stunned silence.

This serves as a mini case study in what so many employees experience in so many workplaces. Every. Single. Day. This worker took what's inside millions and millions of disgruntled employees and let it all out. He felt so undervalued that he was willing to talk about it openly and without provocation to a complete stranger. And this is to say nothing of the fact that there was a long line of customers still waiting to interact with him.

Although this employee said, "They don't pay me enough to care," what he truly communicated reflected his fatalistic perception of his employer:

"*They* don't care."

In a simple-yet-vivid way, this employee articulated what the data says is so pervasive about trust in the workplace today: there are major trust gaps that have a profound effect on the well-being of employees, teams, and organizations. For so many employees, a thousand cuts of distrust will lead to the death of their dream of being a part of a great company. These gaps ultimately influence the way trust is established and built with the customer or the people the organization is serving.

When employees don't have trust in their leaders or their organizations, their level of loyalty will only be based on the value they receive from the employer. When there is a gap in trust, the value becomes increasingly transactional. The fast food worker who told my wife how he really felt was communicating the low value he was experiencing based on his hourly rate.

However, what fueled his toxic response was more than just pay. Every disgruntled customer, every stressful interaction with a manager, every shift that drags on only adds more pressure to his perception of value and his willingness to stay employed or compulsion to walk away.

Despite the dollar amount, the *value* of the paycheck he receives every two weeks gets lower and lower as the trust gap gets wider and wider.

What was most striking to me about this employee's declaration of distrust was that it turned into damaging behavior for the company's brand. He became a very effective marketing manager of one. During the most important activity of any organization—a personal interaction with the customer—his distrust in the company sowed a seed of distrust in the *customer*. The lack of care that he was experiencing translated into a lack of care for the company and a lack of care for that company's customers. At its core, this is trust-breaking behavior.

And this behavior at scale is incredibly costly for an organization.

The solution to building trust is not just to pay the worker more. *Only* paying workers more ultimately falls short because it is an incomplete trust-building strategy. The gap in perception of trustworthiness between leadership and workers will widen into a chasm, especially if profits are the only indicator of success for the leader.

Pawns are expendable when profit is king.

Because these trust gaps are not just one-time experiences, and because they are commonly encountered for both customers and employees, I realized it is essential to dimensionalize this troubling reality. So, I partnered with Kurt Bartolich, someone I trust implicitly, to do a deep dive into organizational trust.

Kurt is the founder and CEO of BrandCertain, a brand strategy company that uses cutting-edge survey methodology and sound data to advise organizations about vitally important decisions related to how they are living out their singular brand truth. Kurt has been gathering national survey data on brands for years, and he offered me the opportunity to add organizational trust questions to his survey. Together, we developed the *National Survey on Brand and Trust* and distributed the survey to over 1,800 participants nationally.

The *National Survey on Brand and Trust* sheds light on various concerning realities taking place in workplaces across every industry. We found data that was both very compelling and very troubling. We also found the results helpful and hopeful because the process revealed specific, tactical things that can be implemented right away (along with things that need to be done away with) in organizations to strengthen trust.

One data point with profound implications that immediately rose to the surface was that leaders rated their own level of trustworthiness 31% *higher* than how employees with no leadership responsibilities rated leader trustworthiness in their organization. This data implies that the further away an employee is from being a decision-maker or influencer in an organization, the more they will distrust the leaders and the organization.

Again, that reflects a 31% gap in trust.

Imagine the good that could occur for the organization if that trust gap was reduced by 5%, 10%, 25%. Imagine the time saved and money saved, the headaches and the heartaches prevented. Imagine retaining the many great employees who left "without reason."

Imagine how the trajectory of an entire organization would change if it took intentional steps to move the workplace culture needle from toxic to trustworthy.

Marcus Buckingham, in his book *First, Break All of the Rules*, rightly said, "People leave managers, not companies."[1] People leave managers who create or perpetuate trust gaps.

Our research further highlighted the troubling effects of the trust gap. We found that trust, unfortunately, is crumbling in every type of organization—no matter the size, no matter the mission, and no matter the location.

In fact, 51% of employees don't have a high level of trust for their leaders. And when surveying the attitudes of those employees compared to employees who have a high level of trust for their leaders, both employee loyalty and employee willingness to refer the company to others drops by 66%.

And half of employees (two-thirds in medium-sized organizations) indicated they aren't likely to work as hard when they don't trust the leaders. Three in five leaders feel the same way.

Employee loyalty, advocacy, work ethic, and job satisfaction all suffer when there is a gap in trust. Of course, the larger the organization, the more dramatic the effect can be.

Trust will not automatically scale on its own, but a trust gap most certainly will.

If you've never experienced a toxic work culture, you're either lucky or lying. A toxic work culture takes root and flourishes in the shadowy gaps where trust could thrive instead.

The MIT Sloan management review states that there are five attributes that contribute to a toxic work culture. They include:

1. Level of disrespect
2. Non-inclusivity
3. Being unethical
4. A cutthroat attitude
5. Abusive behavior[2]

Now imagine each of these attributes as five tiny seeds that get planted within an organization. The seed takes root in the fertile soil of confusing communication, constant drama, and ongoing lack of clarity. Day after day, week after week, and year after year, the seeds of these toxic trees become stronger and taller. Seeds become saplings and saplings mature into trees. Fruit from those trees begins to form—fruit that is consumed by everyone in the organization, along with its customers. That fruit becomes the steady diet of everyone in the organization, and more seeds are planted as a result.

Of course, no one sets out to create and cultivate a toxic workplace. Toxic work environments are the result of individual decisions, attitudes and behaviors of distrust that add up over time. If left unchecked, the organization is left with the perilous process of trying to daily pave a clear path through a dark and dangerous forest of toxicity.

Who would want to work for an organization like that?

Every day another seed is planted, the trust gap is widened, and the resources of time, money, and people move to managing this reality instead of fully carrying out the mission of the organization. Days, weeks, years, and decades pass. Good profits or a good job market minimize the need to grapple with the challenges of the current gap. Worse yet, profits sink and it's both costly and time-consuming to replace people. If left unattended or consistently deprioritized, the organization moves towards toxicity. People will leave toxic work cultures. And, if an organization is unwilling to take the necessary steps to close the trust gap, people *should* leave toxic work cultures.

How challenging is it to draw other people into being fans of your organization or your brand if there is a gap in trust between the leader and the frontline employees? An internal gap in trust will be felt by the people the organization serves. As my friend and fellow researcher Kurt has always told me, "Brands are built from the inside out." Trust is also built from the inside out.

Your organization can be committed to actually measuring the gap between the frontline employee and their leader. This is the first step in addressing things like customer loyalty, employee retention, or employee productivity.

There needs to be a common language of trust and a commitment to consistently wrestle with the challenging organizational dynamics with a proven and helpful framework. Every individual in your organization needs to be consistently held accountable for internalizing and living out the prioritization of trust. Your team needs you to have a heightened sensitivity to the trust gap. Organizational trust can become a stand alone key performance indicator when you accurately and consistently address gaps in the perception of trust. This requires intentionality and discipline.

Ultimately, the trust gap robs not just an organization, but each of its employees of reaching and operating at their full potential. The roots of distrust go deeper than the visible consequences, and these effects are not always immediate. Just as water can erode the strongest of stones given enough time, the trust gap, if unaddressed, can carve deep scars into the foundation of an organization, leading to vulnerabilities that might not be evident at first glance. And as these vulnerabilities manifest, the organization encounters even more profound challenges—challenges that, if ignored, threaten to undermine everything it stands for.

It's important to delve into these deepening concerns and learn how a neglected trust gap can lead an organization into treacherous terrain.

CHAPTER 2
WHEN THE TRUST GAP GETS PERSONAL

The first time I really felt the presence of a trust gap was visceral.

It was the first time my stomach had ever felt this way: knotted with a burning, gnawing pain that felt never-ending. The unsettling aching was only relieved once I finally fell asleep at night. But that relief was temporary.

As soon as my eyes opened in the morning, I was reminded once again of this particular stress and its incredible grip on me. Antacids brought no relief.

I was deep into a toxic workplace dynamic with someone on my team at work. Every conversation with this individual left me feeling like red-hot stomach juices were lapping up high into my throat, reminding me that something was very wrong with every breath I took. The up and down emotions of each one-on-one conversation, the anxiety of every team meeting, and the stress of not feeling equipped to handle this challenging situation led to inescapable physical pain deep in my gut. It was exhausting and maddening, and I felt shame for even feeling it at all. I was the leader. I was supposed to be *better than this.*

I didn't understand how to make sense of the trust gap that plagued my work relationship with this team member. And because of that, it felt like a workplace game of charades every-day. While juggling everything else in my life, work had become a game of keeping my facial expression and tone of voice calm and relaxed while trying to ignore a screaming ulcer and mental divide.

And it went on for months. This toxic workplace dynamic was a low point in my career. I wasn't able to leave my ulcer on my desk on Friday afternoon and pick it up on Monday. The ulcer felt like it was as deep as my soul and impossible to heal. It negatively affected my relationship with my wife and my kids.

It took some time to realize that the ulcer I had developed was in large part a result of a never-ending toxic workplace dynamic. It was a physical manifestation of dread.

As I speak to more audiences and walk alongside more clients, I am constantly reminded that my experience was far from unique. Unfortunately, the ulcer-inducing dread I felt in that toxic workplace is an all too common reality for many people.

Recently, I gave a lunch-hour keynote speech on the topic of trust. As I often do, I asked the audience of roughly 70 people to engage in a simple exercise.

I began with a request: "I'd like for you to write down the initials of the person that you trust the least in a current or past workplace on a piece of paper."

Though hesitant at first, these leaders ultimately embraced the challenge. They translated complex, personal emotions into just two letters. My goal was for each person to move from being a passive participant, sitting and getting information, to assuming a more active role, one that begins a process of discovery. That starts with self-reflection.

For many leaders present, this was the first time they had ever been asked to specifically identify—or even intentionally *think* about—the person to whom they would be the most hesitant about entrusting important things. In the end, there were 70 unique sets of initials sitting on the tables before us.

The implications were vast. This was a moment of reflection and a moment of reckoning.

When I initiate this exercise, I typically have to encourage people with two things. First, I almost always have to remind participants to write *only* one set of initials. Second, I make a point to mention that if the person seated next to a participant is their most untrustworthy selection, cover the paper or choose another set of initials.

This lunchtime keynote was no different. As I said these things, nervous laughter fluttered throughout the room. I could feel tense emotions building pressure like a hot tea kettle whistling as it approaches a boil. I encouraged everyone to look at the initials again, this time for several seconds. Then, I asked the audience to share with the room the core emotion they were experiencing. A few people started squirming in their seats. Some sat perfectly still. Others looked around to see who would be the first to speak. Things were about to get real.

After a few moments, a courageous audience member decided to step up and air out the raw emotion they were still carrying with them when simply *thinking* about working with their selected, untrustworthy person.

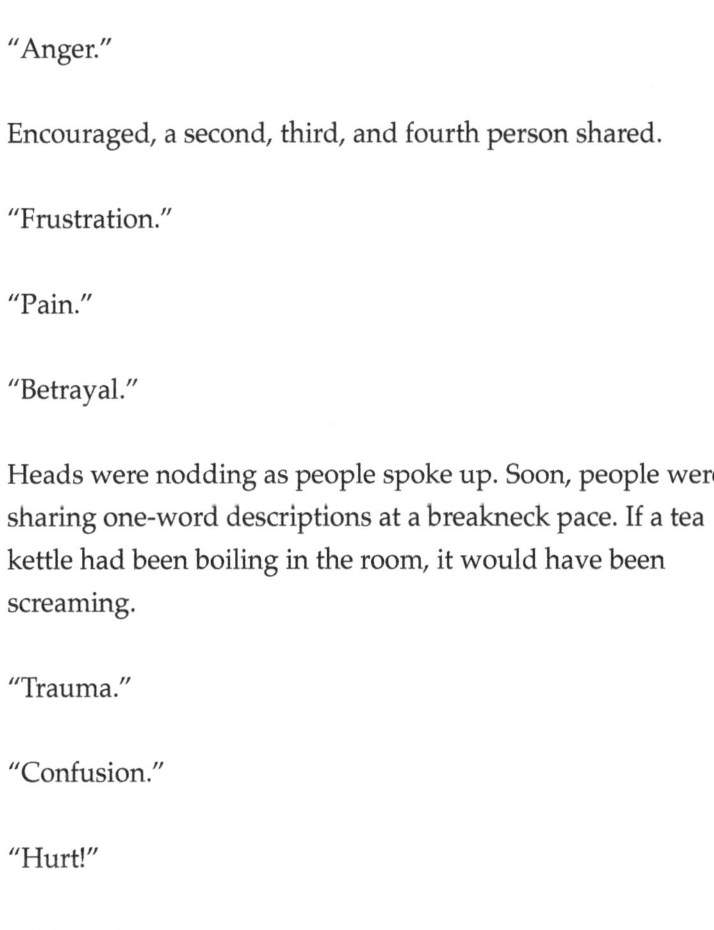

"Anger."

Encouraged, a second, third, and fourth person shared.

"Frustration."

"Pain."

"Betrayal."

Heads were nodding as people spoke up. Soon, people were sharing one-word descriptions at a breakneck pace. If a tea kettle had been boiling in the room, it would have been screaming.

"Trauma."

"Confusion."

"Hurt!"

"Exhaustion."

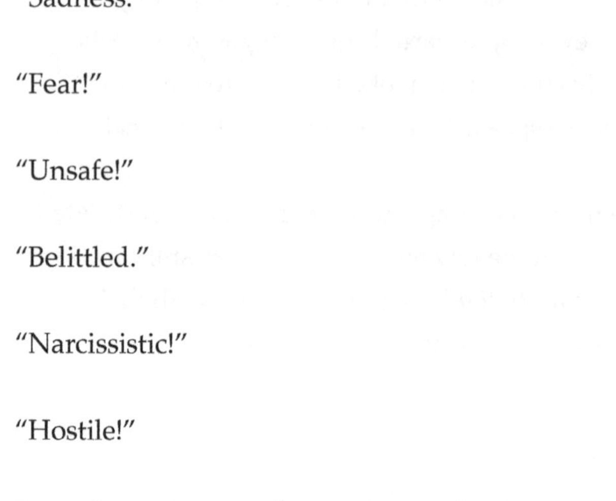

"Sadness."

"Fear!"

"Unsafe!"

"Belittled."

"Narcissistic!"

"Hostile!"

Empathy and sympathy combatted the tension as people shared from their heart and courageously voiced very personal and emotional past experiences. We were only a few minutes into the keynote and I could sense that people were leaning in to support their fellow marketplace leaders in the room. Although everyone's specific experience was different, there was an undeniable commonality of emotion. Each individual had personally been deeply marked by a trust gap.

And then, to my left, and with a clear and resolute voice, one of the audience members unleashed a word nobody was expecting.

"Murder!"

The room went silent.

Now, as an extroverted, Type A, Enneagram 1, Myers-Briggs ESTJ, High D on the DISC Profile, Communications Major and frequent public speaker, I'm rarely at a loss for words (for better or for worse). But at that moment, I stood in shocked silence. My mind was racing with questions:

- "Did that person just say *murder*?"
- "What should *I* say?"
- "How should I say it?"
- "When should I start speaking?"
- *"What just happened?"*

I remember physically taking two steps backward as I let the emotion of that word settle. The only word I could think of that adequately addressed the situation and the emotions that were now weighing heavy on the room was "visceral." It was a moment that crystallized yet again a deep society-wide need to take action on strengthening trust.

So, although we are not physically in the same room together, I'd like to offer the same challenge for you. Instead of reading this as a third party observer, I want you to become an active participant. Write down the initials of the person, either in a current workplace context or a past one, that you trust the least.

Look at those initials and reflect for several seconds on what is surfacing in your mind and in your soul. Under those letters, record your core emotion.

When negative core emotions haunt us, our entire being is affected: physical, social, psychological, vocational, and perhaps even spiritual. Deeply concerning workplaces that go unchecked will ultimately spiral towards toxicity and begin to manifest in both subtle and dramatic ways.

Cynicism, micro-management, quiet quitting, miscommunication, declining loyalty, weak advocacy, high turnover, low productivity, promotions without raises, disappearing pensions, whisper-level conversations, not being heard, office bullies, absolutely endless emails, text messages requesting that you respond to an email, identities wrapped up in job titles, employee of the month initiatives that devalue everyone else, ineffective solutions entrenched in the status quo, satisfaction surveys with no follow-up, pervasive distraction and lack of motivation, the absence of developmental pathways, uncertainty about job security, poor training and coaching, and meeting after meeting after meeting *after meeting where little is actually said and nothing is actually done.*

Deeply concerning workplace environments will also affect critical key performance indicators that will start to show up on month-end and annual reports. This includes, but is not limited to, increased employee turnover, decreased employee productivity, slumping sales, declining employee satisfaction surveys, consistently missed deadlines, and declining net promoter scores—not to mention personal (and organizational) ulcers.

The fact is, low-trust environments should evoke deep concern from leaders, teams, and organizations. For leaders, these spiraling indicators can feel overwhelming, isolating, and even embarrassing. For teams, these indicators can be unsettling, demoralizing, stressful, and unclear. And for organizations, these same indicators can be uncomfortable, gossip-inducing, tenuous, and tremendously taxing. If any of the above workplace conditions are part of your current reality and are causing you deep concern, you are not alone.

And there *is* a solution.

Let's flip the script and evoke a different trust emotion. Repeat the same exercise, but this time, write down the initials of a person you have the *highest* level of trust for.

Just as before, take a moment to study those initials, then write down your core emotion beneath them.

Visualize the person in your mind that you have experienced this high level of trust for. What reaction do you notice in your mind and body? If you don't have a smile on your face reflecting on that person, you most likely have very positive thoughts and gratitude welling up inside of you. And there's a reason for that.

Trustworthy people bring life to an organization. They have an uncanny ability to navigate challenging issues with kindness and directness. They bring a resolve to focus on working through challenges in a sophisticated, forward-thinking, and inspiring way. They are unflappable and consistent in how they show up, and they bring a refreshing energy to both hallway conversations and formal meetings.

Trustworthy individuals are highly competent in many areas of their work. They are also problem solvers who use challenging moments as catalytic opportunities. They tend to show a high level of care for both their coworkers and their customers. Their attitude drives their actions, and their behaviors are energizing. Words of confidence and hope are spoken from them and about them.

Josue Valles, a talented content creator on LinkedIn, has a powerful list of trust words:

- Approved
- Authentic
- Authority
- Backed
- Because
- Best
- Bulletproof
- Certified
- Clockwork
- Endorsed
- Foolproof
- Genuine
- Guaranteed
- Ironclad
- Money-back
- No risk
- Official
- Proven
- Refund
- Reliable
- Research
- Science
- Study
- Surefire
- Tested
- World-class[1]

Are these the words that are being spoken in your organization? Is this the vocabulary of your team? If you were to record every conversation you have this next week at work, would your actual words and the words listed above be similar? How do the words above compare to the day-to-day conversations occurring in meetings, hallways, and break rooms in your organization?

One of the most challenging outcomes of workplaces struggling with trust is a lack of employee engagement. Employee engagement and employee experience are hot-button items. There's an industry being built around employee experience because organizations know that when the experience for employees is engaging and outstanding, key success indicators will follow.

The Society of Human Resource Managers (SHRM) has a helpful comparison of the behaviors associated with engagement and disengagement:

> **Engagement Behaviors**: Optimistic, team-oriented, goes above and beyond, solution-oriented, selfless, shows a passion for learning, passes along credit but accepts blame.
>
> **Disengaged Behaviors**: Pessimistic, self-centered, high absenteeism, negative attitude, egocentric, focus on monetary worth, accepts credit but passes along blame.[2]

Think of the times in your career when you have worked with a team member, a leader, or a team that displays any of the above disengaged behaviors. Think about how draining, dramatic, and demoralizing it was. The amount of energy that goes into managing disengaged employees is staggering and damaging to people personally and collectively. We've probably all had times in our professional lives when we have been disengaged —I know I certainly have. It's a terrible feeling; the value of time spent doing the job that I felt disengaged in was off-balance. The days go by slowly, the work doesn't have the same purpose, relationships are strained, and it's easy to become hypersensitive and cynical. Disengaged employees are circling the workplace drain, and it's challenging to recover from this all-too-common work dynamic.

It's true that behavior affects our attitudes, but as my friend and fellow researcher Kurt Bartolich says, "Attitude drives behavior."

You'll see from the research results discussed throughout this book that trust is the primary driver of the attitudes of leaders, teams, and employees. As such, there are two important truths to be mindful of when thinking about engagement in your organization.

First, the root of the attitude that drives the behavior of an engaged, healthy, thriving employee is trust.

Second, the root of the attitude that drives the behavior of a disengaged, unhealthy, flailing employee is distrust.

You don't have to *make* it personal, because it *is* personal. And if you or anyone on your team forgets this truth, remind them with the exercises above. Grapple with and personally resolve to work hard every day to close the trust gap.

CHAPTER 3
EPIDEMIC OF DISTRUST

I was hosting a Zoom call and asked an executive from an extremely recognizable national brand, "Are you concerned that there are some gaps in trust among team members in your company?"

Their response?

"Yes, there are definitely some challenges we are facing related to trust issues that are impacting our workplace culture."

I appreciated her honesty, and I was excited about the potential opportunity to help a lot of people in their organization. "Would your company be interested in measuring the level of trust your employees have for leadership and fellow team members, in order to develop a plan to strengthen trust?" I asked.

The executive paused for a moment and then shrugged. "Actually, probably not, because honestly we're making too much money to *really* worry about improving employee trust."

I had to pick up my jaw off the floor.

I do have to give this company credit for being honest enough to express what many organizations would never admit: the trust gaps in their organizations are ever-present, but too many other things (like profits) are shoving it too far down the priority list to address it in meaningful and sustainable ways.

Sadly, they are willing to sacrifice trust at the altar of their own profits. They don't care about the long-term damage, and they don't care about the risk of destroying their internal culture. They're so shortsighted with their balance sheet that they are willing to ignore individuals—and ultimately the long-term health and wellbeing of the organization—because of their current "success." The tragic reality of this statement means the trust gaps will continue and likely widen until something catastrophic happens—employees leave in a mass exodus, a product fails and tanks the profits, outdated policies and practices lead to a data breach, or a company's lack of teamwork and innovation stalls their progress and they get leapfrogged by their competition.

Listen closely to the language of distrust that may be surfacing in your organization, and listen to words coming out of your own mouth first:

"That's just the way it is."

"We've always done it that way."

"That's not my problem to solve."

"That'll never happen."

"Don't rock the boat, because it will mean more work for all of us."

"I don't know, go ask someone who cares."

"They don't listen to me anyway."

"Hopefully that leader will retire soon so we can make the changes we need to."

Multiply this reality times a million, repeat it every single day, and you have an epidemic of distrust. The definition of an epidemic is "affecting or tending to affect a disproportionately large number of individuals within a population, community, or region at the same time; characterized by very widespread growth."[1] The risk of an epidemic is widespread and uncontrollable disease. And as with any transmissible disease, if you ignore it, it will only get worse.

Perhaps you are experiencing positive momentum in your organization. Things are working. Your performance indicator dashboard is healthy, and things "feel good" in your workplace culture. It's vital that you identify the source of that positive momentum to ensure that trust gaps do not open. Self-reflect regularly on questions like these:

- What is driving the attitudes and behaviors that are causing your organization to be healthy?
- Who are your trust champions and how do you ensure you are listening and responding to them on a regular basis?
- Who are the people that you've got some concerns about and how are you addressing those concerns?
- What are the policies or the practices that don't make sense and how are you prioritizing evaluation and possible revision?
- How do you keep the trust gaps closed not just for the near term, but how does this become your long-term reality?

You might be concerned that the epidemic of distrust that you know exists in other organizations is now on the horizon for yours. You are operating with present-day pressures and strapped down by outdated legacy policies that create drag on your company. Like a submarine with torpedoes approaching it, there is something pinging on your internal radar. You are not able to articulate and take action on what you are sensing, but you know it's there. The temperature in your organization is rising, and there is an early onset of infection that is beginning to grow in different areas of your company culture.

You are not alone.

A 2021 Pew National survey found deep distrust among various groups: from medical scientists to the military, police officers to school principals, scientists to retail and entertainment, religious leaders to business leaders and the government. Here's a breakdown of the startling data:

% of U.S. adults who have "a great deal" of confidence in the following groups to act in the best interest of the public:

- Medical Scientists: 29%
- Scientists: 29%
- The Military: 25%
- Police Officers: 20%
- Public School Principals: 14%
- Religious Leaders: 12%
- Journalists: 6%
- Business Leaders: 4%
- Elected Officials: 2%[2]

As if the numbers weren't shocking enough, the year-over-year trend is even more shocking. With every group surveyed, the percentage of U.S. adults who have a great deal of confidence in those groups acting in the best interest of the public was lower than the year before. The research also revealed a concerning malaise toward this epidemic of distrust.[3] It's one thing if something is wrong. But it's deeply troubling when something is obviously wrong and there's no sense of urgency to fix it. This kind of behavior screams the statement, "It's just the way it is."

In another staggering study conducted by Pew Research titled "Trust and Distrust in America," only 25% of those surveyed felt that Americans' level of confidence in each other (or lack thereof) is a "very big problem."

% of Americans who say the following is a very big problem:

- Drug addiction: 70%
- Affordability of health care: 67%
- Ethics in government: 67%
- Affordability of education: 63%
- The gap between rich and poor: 51%
- Violent crime: 49%
- Climate change: 46%
- Racism: 40%
- Illegal immigration: 38%
- Terrorism: 34%
- **Level of confidence in each other: 25%**
- Job opportunities for all: 25%[4]

Even though interpersonal distrust is not seen as a top-ranking issue, there is an undercurrent of desire to address the problem of interpersonal trust. 70% agree with another statement, "Americans' low trust in each other makes it harder to solve many of the country's problems." That contrasts with the 29% who back a different assertion, "The country's problems would be just as hard to solve even if Americans' trust in each other was higher."[5] Of course, the pandemic and all of the social division that has occurred since then has only deepened the level of distrust. This distrust is carried with us wherever we go, especially in the place we spent the majority of our waking hours: our workplaces.

In 2022, a new phrase was coined to describe the mass exodus of workers from their jobs: *The Great Resignation*. Shockwaves were sent through every industry during the Great Resignation to the tune of 50.5 million people quitting their jobs in that year alone. The confluence of a positive job market combined with negative workplace culture created the perfect storm for tens of millions of people voting with their feet and leaving their companies.[6]

Let the number 50.5 million sink in for a moment. That number represents nearly ⅓ of the American workforce resigning from their jobs in 2022. And, for those who resigned that year and moved to a different job, they entered a new workplace culture fraught with the anxiety of a pandemic coupled with massive shifts in the job market. These were tremendously anxious times for the labor market that will be felt for many years.

Our research shows the troubling effects of distrust within organizations and the dramatic impact it has on key performance indicators. When looking specifically at the 18% of employees who have little to no trust in their leaders, only 16% of them have a high level of loyalty to their organization and only 12% are likely to refer that organization to others. Consider the effect of one-fifth of your workforce actively resisting supporting your organization at any given time. It's analogous to a sailboat trying to make progress with its anchor down and dragging along the bottom of the ocean floor. No amount of wind in the sails or expertise from the crew can overcome the drag the boat is experiencing.

Countless budget dollars for companies large and small across all industries are allocated towards "employee engagement," but data shows only a stale effect. Not only does there continue to be a troublingly low number of employees who are engaged (21%), there is also a high (and even more troubling) level of employees who are ACTIVELY disengaged (19%).

Employee engagement is the fuel of an organization. Imagine the fuel tank of a race car that contains 21% properly mixed fuel, 19% bad fuel, and 60% standard gasoline. Once on the racetrack, the effects of non-optimized fuel would quickly become evident. The race car would soon be lapped, becoming a liability and endangering other drivers on the track.

And, as we have seen from the data, this epidemic of distrust is agnostic. The epidemic has no concern for industry, company, age or tenure of employees, sophistication of technology, geographic region, or company size. The disease of distrust silently and invisibly moves in and out of meeting rooms, hallway conversations, email chains, and Slack channels, and it manifests itself in countless ways. The epidemic of distrust exists within organizations that are stagnating and in those that are growing. And if left unchecked, the epidemic of distrust moves from troubling to toxic.

Toxic. This single word is packed with implications and emotions and describes the terrible effects of distrust.

Marcel Schwantes, founder of Leadership from the Core, shares "Six Toxic Phrases That Should Never Come Out of a Leader's Mouth":

1. "I don't need anybody's opinion. This is the direction we're headed."
2. "I'm not responsible for that—go blame someone else."
3. "I don't need to get trained, I know everything there is to know."
4. "That's why I hired you. Figure it out for yourself."
5. "It is what it is."

6. "I can't do this for you, so don't even bother asking again."[7]

Whether you actually hear those phrases coming out of a leader's mouth or they demonstrate them with their actions, they are indicators of a mindset that does irreparable harm. When this mindset goes viral, it will get adopted by others and become a movement. As the movement grows, it gains momentum. As momentum continues, it becomes the norm. As norms are cemented, they shape the values and the ethos of the organization. Particles of distrust get distributed throughout the company, and people breathe them in without even knowing. It becomes part of the new environment and atmosphere.

This can be especially difficult for leaders who find themselves in a new season of influence or are stepping into this atmosphere for the first time. It can feel like walking into an emergency room on a busy Saturday night, trying to make sense of how to help dozens of sick patients without the support of other doctors and nurses. This kind of organizational triage is impossible to sustain long-term.

One of the most recognizable symbols in our culture is the biohazard symbol. You see it in hospitals, in medical clinics, in bathrooms where there are sharps disposal containers. It's a warning that if you don't know what you are stepping towards or if you don't have the necessary equipment with you, you should turn the other way. It's a symbol that represents the harmful source of some type of insidious agent, and it should stop you in your tracks and prompt you to move quickly towards safety.

The biohazard symbol, developed in 1966 by Charles L. Baldwin and Robert S. Runkle, was a solution to a wide range of symbols used to warn people of infectious biological agents. When asked why he co-created the symbol, Charles Baldwin said, "We wanted something that was memorable but meaningless, so we could educate people as to what it means." There are four circles of meaning represented by the symbol:

1. **Agent:** The pathogen capable of producing infection or infectious disease
2. **Source:** The host from which the pathogen originated
3. **Transmission:** The process of how the pathogen infects the host
4. **Host:** The organism the pathogen infects[8]

"Biological hazards, also known as biohazards, refer to biological substances that pose a threat to the health of living organisms, primarily that of humans. This can include medical waste or samples of a microorganism, viruses, or toxins (from a biological source) that can affect human health. Symbolized by a striking medallion of curving, curlicue scepters, the sinister nature of the biohazard is evoked by the sharp and pointed nature of the otherwise round symbol."[9]

The sharp points and the disjointed nature of the overlapping circles not touching each other are caused by the numerous *gaps*. It's a powerful symbol because it screams danger without using words. It looks like some type of weapon used in ancient warfare. This symbol is recognizable from far away, and it warns us even if we don't know the source or significance of the biohazard.

When we are in a biohazard environment, we have four options: 1) move away from the current environment, 2) stay in place and run the risk of getting sick from the biohazard, 3) acquire and use the proper equipment to stay safe in the dangerous environment, or 4) bring in an outside source of help to remove the biohazard altogether.

The biohazard symbol is striking because it's the exact shape of a Venn diagram that has been fractured, disjointed, and altered completely because of the gaps in the circles. The Venn diagram is a well-known tool commonly used to show the interaction of three parts of a system or process:

The three independent circles are brought together to form a new and better interrelated system. The place all three circles intersect is called the nexus. The nexus would not be possible without the convergence of the three circles. But when the circles break, when gaps begin to form, the system becomes unstable and vulnerable, creating a toxic hazard.

If there were a sign posted on the front door of your company office, would it be a biohazard symbol or a Venn diagram of trust? If your employees assessed your current culture on a sliding scale, would it lean towards toxic or trustworthy?

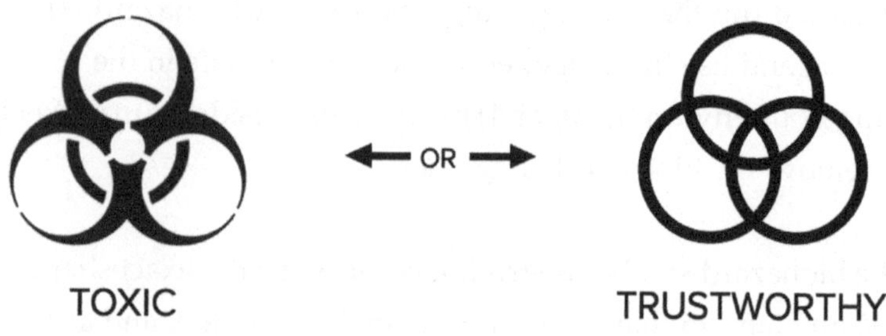

The gaps in trust are what make it toxic. The gaps in trust make it a hazard. The gaps in trust, if left unaddressed, will become an epidemic.

Distrust is the deep root of the status quo, and organizations will naturally become entrenched in the efficiency of "that's just the way it is." So, every leader has a choice. Every employee has a choice. You have a choice. You can lean in, speak up, and take a stand against the hazardous behaviors that are making your company sick. Or, you can continue to live in the midst of an epidemic of distrust.

If the biohazard symbol best represents your current reality, the work you do may feel hopeless. But even in the midst of an ever-deepening epidemic of distrust, there is hope. There is a way out. It's within every individual's and organization's power to do something about this silent workplace culture killer. It is possible for you to lean into your influence and authority to engage in consistent, repeatable behavior to close the trust gaps. It starts by relentlessly evaluating your current reality, adopting a proven trust framework, and taking action to close the gaps in trust.

There is light at the end of this tunnel. There is an evidence-based framework of trust that is clarifying, practical, and easy to use and remember. And I can't wait to share that framework with you in a few chapters. But before we do that, let's understand more clearly the power of trust.

CHAPTER 4
THE POWER OF TRUST

I slowly shuffled into my dark office to begin my typical early morning routine at 5:00 a.m., and I instinctively flipped on the light switch. Warm light instantly filled our main floor study. The quiet morning hours are a refuge for me: my favorite, well-seasoned, brown leather chair, hot coffee in a familiar ceramic mug, peace, quiet, clarity, and focused productivity. My early morning hours are my "best hours" primarily because they are fueled by coffee at a rate of about one cup per thirty minutes.

Less than an hour into my routine, the power suddenly went out. The lamp in the corner of my office went dark, the clock blinked off, and the soothing hum of the furnace instantly stopped. Dead silence. That is, except for the wind howling outside our study window. There was a winter storm raging through the Midwest like a freight train, so I shouldn't have been too surprised by the power outage. The storm system had been forecasted for days, but even with an accurate forecast, it's always a bit unnerving when the power goes out.

Two hours later, with the power still off and the family still in bed, my top priority became a mission where failure was not an option: brave the cold, wind, and snow-covered Midwest roads to get a cup of hot, fresh coffee for my wife, as the Keurig was currently rendered powerless and useless. And, it was one of the few times I could actually justify owning a four-wheel drive truck. Born and raised in Wyoming, winter storms weren't foreign to me, but this was the first time I'd ever risked life and limb for a Venti Pike Place roast.

I accomplished my mission—the coffee was safely acquired and delivered. My wife said (and I quote), "I thank you eternally for getting me coffee this morning." She shared later that she had planned on staying in bed until either the power came on or the coffee magically appeared at her bedside. That was the only highlight of the morning. The storm continued to rage and the power remained off, interrupting and challenging all our typical expectations and routines.

There were copious amounts of speculation, wishful thinking, and assumed expertise by all members of the family about when the power would be turned back on. Concerns escalated as it became clear that our loss of power could move from a minor inconvenience to a more dramatic disruption (like wondering who we would be contacting and staying with later that night). Frustration intensified as accusations surfaced: the "people in charge" hadn't "fixed our problem" yet. My two middle schoolers were particularly restless, saying, "I hate this, my phone won't work and all I want is for the power to be back on."

It was amazing how crippled we felt when we didn't have electricity. As the temperature of the house dropped into the low 60s, our confidence in the electrical grid began declining at the same rate as our elevating concerns.

Organizational trust is like electrical power—you don't realize how much you depend on it until it's gone. Trust, like voltage, is the power that must exist in every organization. Without trust, the "switches" (people, policies, and practices) of a company may be operating sufficiently for a time, but the workplace culture conditions will ultimately worsen. The absence of organizational trust, like the absence of electricity, changes every dynamic of the environment, and if left unchecked, it can become at best concerning and at worst dangerous. Similar to our house on that brutally cold morning, when trust is gone, organizational resistance will begin to overwhelm the system, and a new dynamic, a new narrative, and new challenges will emerge.

There will be copious amounts of spoken and unspoken speculation—and assumed expertise—by all members of the organization about when trust will or won't be restored. Concerns will continue to escalate that the loss of trust could move from a minor inconvenience to a dramatic disruption. Frustration will intensify and accusations will surface because the "people in charge" haven't "fixed the problem" yet. Team members will get restless, saying "I hate this, my situation doesn't work and I just want trust to be restored." Organizational leaders will nervously reflect as they try to navigate the situation: "Isn't it amazing how crippled we feel when we don't have trust?"

Why is organizational trust so powerful? Let's go back to the definition used at the beginning of the book. "Trust is the firm belief in the truth of something." Consider the implications when there is an absence of the firm belief in the truth of something. When something firm becomes fragile. When belief becomes doubt. When truth becomes gibberish, skepticism, and suspicion.

Dennis Jaffe writes:

> Trust makes people feel eager to be part of a relationship or group, with a shared purpose and a willingness to depend on each other. When trust is intact, we will willingly contribute what is needed, not just by offering our presence, but also by sharing our dedication, talent, energy, and honest thoughts on how the relationship or group is working.[1]

When trust is present, hope is present. Hope for success because there are clear expectations and appropriate accountability for each employee. Hope for fulfillment because workplace environmental conditions are optimal for the betterment of teams. Hope for resilience because the current strength of the organization will help to navigate marketplace challenges in the future. Hope for long-term sustainability and viability because the organization is doing things the right way. Hope because the organization is confidently willing to change for the better in the future instead of resisting that change. Hope because the ethos of the organization is fueled by people of integrity, wisdom, creativity, appropriate vulnerability, and strength of character.

Stephen Covey, in his seminal book written over twenty years ago titled *The Speed of Trust: The One Thing That Changes Everything*, beautifully articulates the power of trust:

> There is one thing that is common to every individual, relationship, team, family, organization, nation, economy, and civilization throughout the world—one thing which, if removed, will destroy the most powerful government, the most successful business, the most thriving economy, the most influential leadership, the greatest friendship, the strongest character, the deepest love. On the other hand, if developed and leveraged, that one thing has the potential to create unparalleled success and prosperity in every dimension of life. Yet, it is the least understood, most neglected, and most underestimated possibility of our time. That one thing is trust.[2]

Trust is the lifeblood of an organization. And trust, when mishandled, can be incredibly damaging and costly. It's paradoxical to consider that there are "problems" with trust. But because the stakes are so high with trust, many problems arise when it's mishandled. Here are ten problems that, if left unchecked, will only serve to widen the trust gap.

PROBLEM #1: TRUST IS INCREMENTALLY BUILT, BUT CAN BE INSTANTLY BROKEN.

Like a lightning strike snapping a hundred-year-old tree, organizational trust can be snapped in an instant. One decision, one action, or one moment can completely alter what has taken years to build. The damage becomes widespread when the lightning strike turns into a forest fire.

PROBLEM #2: ONCE TRUST IS GONE, IT WILL NEVER BE THE SAME.

When trust has been broken, a scar will always remain. As a result, the trust dynamic will never be the same. The process of reconciliation, healing, and forgiveness is important. However, efforts deployed to restore trust to *sameness* will remain futile.

PROBLEM #3: TRUST IS HARDER TO RE-BUILD THAN TO BUILD THE FIRST TIME.

Restoring a painting or renovating a house is much harder than beginning with a blank canvas or starting with an empty plot of land. The remnants and the residue of distrust are costly to the process of rebuilding trust.

PROBLEM #4: TRUST IS TREATED AS JUST AN EFFECT INSTEAD OF A CAUSE AND EFFECT.

If the toxic residue of distrust or a widening trust gap is the common catalyst to start thinking about trust, it's simply too late. Trust needs to begin at the headwaters instead of only being addressed downstream.

PROBLEM #5: TRUST DOESN'T DANCE WELL WITH DISTRACTION.

Research shows that we each make 35,000 decisions each day[3] (no wonder I'm ready to go to bed at 9:14 p.m. every night). Every decision we make is an opportunity to take action on closing the trust gap. Trust flails and will ultimately fail when it's not focused.

PROBLEM #6: TRUST REQUIRES ONGOING ATTENTION AND DISCIPLINE.

Even if your team is not starving for trust, your team's thirst for trust should never be fully quenched. Your trust gap radar and your toxic distrust sensor need to be regularly active and highly sensitive, continually scanning conversations, messages, decisions, feedback, policies, and strategies. Every moment presents you with an opportunity to nourish trust within your company.

PROBLEM #7: TRUST IS MORE THAN POSITIONAL.

A mentor and friend of mine named John Newsom wisely shared this axiom with me: "Loyalty may only be positional, but trust is always relational." Our data confirms that truth with assessment results showing high levels of positional loyalty, despite waning levels of trust. Put simply, it's possible to be loyal to someone in a leadership position despite having low levels of relational trust for them. The data also shows that this is not sustainable and that ultimately, this thin veil of loyalty will not be enough for people to stay at the company and remain engaged.

PROBLEM #8: TRUST IS MINIMIZED TO THEORY INSTEAD OF REALIZED THROUGH TACTICS.

Theory is one thing, but being tactical about trust leads to incredibly valuable outcomes. According to Bryan Robinson, Ph.D.:

> Behavioral economists show that trustworthiness leads to higher economic gains and increases in information sharing, openness, fluidity and cooperation in the workplace. Data from Deloitte show that trusted companies outperform their peers by up to 400%, directly correlating with the bottom line. Customers who trust a brand are 88% more likely to buy again. And 79% of employees who trust their employers are more motivated to work and less likely to leave.[4]

Trust must be moved from theory to practice.

PROBLEM #9: TRUST IS RARELY MEASURED AS A KPI.

Because trust is vital, it must also be measurable. A Deloitte LLP analysis, for example, found that three large global companies, each with a market cap of more than $10 billion, lost 20% to 56% of their value—a total of $70 billion—when they breached their stakeholders' trust.[5] Is trust as important to your organization as other key performance indicators like net revenue, conversion rates, website traffic, production efficiency, net promoter and employee satisfaction? If not, it should be. Trust can and must be measured as any other KPI.

PROBLEM #10: TRUST IS THOUGHT OF AS A FLUKE INSTEAD OF A FRAMEWORK.

Because the implications of trust are so incredibly important, the clearer everyone in your organization is about the framework for trust, the more aligned everyone will be about the blueprint for strengthening trust. "The greatest teaching tool at a leaders' disposal is a framework. A framework is a road map for success that is predetermined to be effective in times of crisis."[6] If there is a consistent gap in the understanding or perceptions about what trust is and how to talk about it, there will be a consistent gap in the organization's ability to take action.

When these types of problems persist, your employees will feel far less compelled to contribute, engage, build resilience through the difficult times, or to help actively close the trust gap. When trust is gone, highly disruptive conditions begin to take root. A once powerful organization becomes powerless, resulting in decreased employee productivity, creativity, work ethic, retention, and advocacy. Every person is then forced to choose how they will respond to such a sharp decline in trust.

Some people will leave, and some will stay even though they shouldn't. Some will go into protection mode through overt isolation and deepening of silos. Some will gossip and set up residence in the house of pain. Some will become the company champion of a victim mindset. And some will emerge from the worsening conditions and demonstrate a desire to restore power.

But when the light switches are on and there is no power, don't blame the switches.

Start by restoring the power.

In the same way, when employees are doing what they are told within a workplace culture that is at best concerning and at worst toxic, don't blame them.

Instead, take accountability and start restoring trust.

Trust, like electrical power in a house, should never be assumed, especially when distrust indicators are helping to forecast storms. Trust, like electrical power, must stay on or be restored quickly—at any cost. The BCG Henderson Institute articulates this well: "The business value of trustworthiness is more than monetary: it is becoming increasingly important to a company's very license to operate."[7] The question then becomes: how do leaders, teams, and organizations restore the power of trust? The rest of this book is focused on how to harness the power of trust and move your organization from deep concern to deep, healthy, and sustainable impact.

The power is in your hands.

CHAPTER 5
THE TRUST PROPOSITION

It was the first Saturday in three years that I didn't have a paper, project, or research due for my doctoral program. I had successfully completed the defense of my dissertation and finalized all of the requirements for my program earlier that week. All I needed to do was walk across the stage to receive my diploma. The weight of the world was off my shoulders, and I felt that I had gotten 40% of my life back.

I settled into my favorite living room chair early that Saturday morning, a hot cup of coffee in hand. But two minutes into my well-deserved respite, I thought I felt a drop of liquid land near me. I couldn't confirm it and thought nothing of it until thirty seconds later, when I felt another drip on my right arm.

I looked up to the ceiling that separated the main floor of the house from the second floor where my four children slept. Directly above me was a huge water-stain on the ceiling with dozens of droplets ready to rain down on me. I visualized the room directly above me. Realization turned to horror as I determined the dripping was coming from the kids' bathroom.

I abandoned my nearly full cup of coffee and dashed upstairs to the bathroom to investigate. As I walked inside, I found exactly what I didn't want to find: water everywhere on the floor, a clogged toilet, and the filthy contents of the porcelain bowl reaching up to the rim.

I knew the valve in the tank of the toilet had a very slow leak, but it had never been a major problem. At the same time, I could just envision one of the children pulling down on the toilet handle like it was a casino slot machine, pull after pull until the level of water maxed out the bowl's capacity.

And because I hadn't taken the small valve leak seriously, now my whole family would experience a massive issue that *couldn't* be ignored.

Enough dirty water leaked out throughout the night to reach the edges of the bathroom and permeate into the subfloor. Now, eight hours later, it was dripping onto the living room carpet.

It would have been bad enough if the water had been clean, but the fact that it was dirty made things much more complex. The toxic water took the situation to a new level, and I knew I needed outside help. I reluctantly called my insurance company and explained the situation. They immediately deployed a remediation team. Within an hour there was a huge orange truck backing into my driveway and a crew of remediation workers armed with tools and fans. Absolute chaos was about to descend on our house.

The remediation team shared with me in a much calmer voice than I was currently experiencing in my mind that every surface affected by the leak would need to be removed. They informed me that the situation needed "immediate and comprehensive attention" since the flooding involved contaminated water.

By early that afternoon, the main level of our house was in complete shambles. Carpet and drywall were removed from the affected areas, huge drying fans were running, and thick plastic sheets were hung from the ceiling to enclose the affected area. It took weeks for our house to be put back together, and our stomachs still sink every time we have a toilet malfunction or water leak in our house.

This is analogous to what takes place in an organization with a toxic work culture. A slow drip of mistrust can turn quickly into a major problem that is highly disruptive to the rest of the organization. Room by room, team by team, the effect of a toxic workplace can seep through an organization like water through drywall. Unsuspecting leaders begin to realize the symptoms of an ever-increasing toxic drip in key performance indicators like low employee retention, decreasing employee productivity, slumping employee satisfaction surveys, and low levels of employee loyalty. The environment changes, and the stains of negativity become more prevalent. Day-to-day operations focused on efficiency, engagement, and excellence are replaced with sopping up the crappy messes of an unhealthy organization.

The problem, of course, only worsens when remediation doesn't occur and leadership chooses to live in denial instead.

When prolonged denial becomes the status quo—when there's poison in the water—it may take years to recover. Or, if addressed too late, it may never recover at all. Decades-old water damage in a home makes floors weak, uneven, and dangerous. And people can't thrive when they don't feel safe. It's hard to focus or be creative when the ceiling is leaking toxic water on you and the floors beneath you are stained and precarious.

Real leaders take responsibility and courageously commit to addressing toxic trouble. They have the power to help the organization close the gap by moving the organization from toxic to trustworthy.

Imagine what would have happened to the health of my family, the condition of our house, and our budget if I had allowed that leak to spread its toxicity into our walls, onto our floors, and on top of our furniture. I could have denied the reality of the problem, but that would have only made things worse to the point of catastrophe.

I had to face the facts, as hard as they were to face, and take the necessary steps to address and fix the situation for the well-being of my family. I could have been upset at my children, but I was the adult here. I had always known that toilet had an issue. This disaster wasn't my kids' fault—it was mine. And it was my responsibility to fix the leak, remove the soiled items, and ultimately replace all of the carpet and drywall.

I wasn't doing a cost-benefit analysis or thinking about a value proposition; I was only thinking about restoring our house to a place where my family could trust that it was once again safe.

Because trust is worth more than anything, I had to spend to secure it.

Ask any business leader what a value proposition is, and they will probably be able to articulate it well. According to the Corporate Finance Institute:

> A value proposition is a promise of value stated by a company that summarizes how the benefit of the company's product or service will be delivered, experienced, and acquired. Essentially, a value proposition specifies what makes the company's product or service attractive, why a customer should purchase it, and how the value of the product or service is differentiated from similar offerings.[1]

As consumers, we are constantly looking for the value proposition. Is the product or service *worth* what I am going to pay? The worth of something is translated to how we *value* that thing. Michael Lanning first coined the term "value proposition" in the late 1980s while he was being interviewed by Brian Carroll. Afterward, Carroll shared his key takeaways on what a value proposition should do:

1. Drive, but not be equated with, your message. It should be an internal articulation, to be echoed by your message.
2. Focus on the specific, measurable experiences customers will derive by doing business with you.
3. Be reflected across and influence your entire business, not just your messaging, marketing, and sales.[2]

One of the best examples of a value proposition in the work that I do regards appointment scheduling. During the startup phase of the company I founded, TrustCentric™, I wore all the hats of the business. One of the things that I found took a significant amount of my time and energy was scheduling appointments throughout the week. Since many of my appointments take place via Zoom, the never-ending game of calendar availability ping pong, coupled with setting up each appointment, was a serious drain on my time.

Time is a vital currency, and there are some weeks where I have dozens of appointments. Those appointments, multiplied by the time it takes to coordinate schedules, were having a serious impact on my business. Then, I found Calendly, a $12-per-month scheduling app (cue angels singing). It revolutionized a critical operational reality of my business, and it's worth far more than what I pay each month. The value proposition with Calendly is *very high*.

The concept of a value proposition is well known and understood. But the first time I ever thought about the concept of a *trust proposition* was when I was knee-deep in my doctoral research.

I was attending a meeting in the faculty lounge on a college campus. The person I was meeting with was a very accomplished researcher for one of the most dynamic and respected education foundations in the country. Her work specifically focused on trends, challenges, and opportunities in higher education. During her many years of research in this space, she had met with over two thousand leaders of higher education institutions.

We were well into the conversation when I asked a question that was pivotal for my paradigm on trust. With my Executive MBA experience still top of mind from a couple of years prior, where so much of my work was focused on building, maintaining, and leveraging a value proposition, I asked, "Of all of the colleges and universities that you have met with, how many conversations ultimately revolved around the concept of value proposition?"

Without hesitation, she replied, "All of them."

She continued, "Every meeting I have had, whether it be with the college president, provost, dean, vice president, or board member always centered around their value proposition—how do we communicate and deliver on the promise that the price being paid and the commitment of time for students will be *worth* it."

I followed up with this question: "In all of your conversations with those same leaders of these institutions, how many of them spoke about the vital need to strengthen their *trust proposition*?"

As I said the phrase "trust proposition," I realized it was not only the first time I had ever put those two words together, it was also the first time I had ever *heard* that phrase. But in the course of our conversation, it was a spur-of-the-moment way for me to differentiate trust from value, and connect this new phrase—"trust proposition"—to a ubiquitous business concept of a value proposition.

She paused, as if she was scanning through thousands of hours of conversations in her mind. She then went from leaning forward with her hands on the table to sitting back fully in her chair, as if settling into the response she was about to give.

She looked at me and said, "Never."

It was a watershed moment for me. Together, we began to unpack the difference between value and trust. She reflected on how value was the primary driver of each conversation she had with most leaders. She lamented the fact that prioritizing trust was noticeably absent. In essence, she was saying there was a tremendous amount of energy spent trying to fill the trust gap with value proposition tactics, and it wasn't working.

That meeting made me realize there needed to be a new way to think about and talk about trust.

I'm deeply grateful for that conversation. I'm also deeply grateful for a seminal study that was conducted by three researchers in the early 2000s. Deepak Sirdeshmukh, Jagdip Singh, and Barry Sabol published a research study in the *Journal of Marketing* in 2002 called "Consumer Trust, Value, and Loyalty in Relational Exchanges." This was the framework I used to process my data for my doctoral work. It has been foundational for how I work alongside teams, leaders, organizations to help them understand and take action on trust. These researchers were specifically looking at the dynamics of a value proposition that is either being gained or lost within the organization and how it was effecting relational loyalty. Their research focused on the airline industry and the retail industry, and they identified three vital factors of trust that significantly affect value and loyalty. We'll do a much deeper dive on this later in the book.

For the consumer experience, these researchers shared a sequence that doesn't start with value—it *starts with trust*. Here is that sequence in its simplest form:

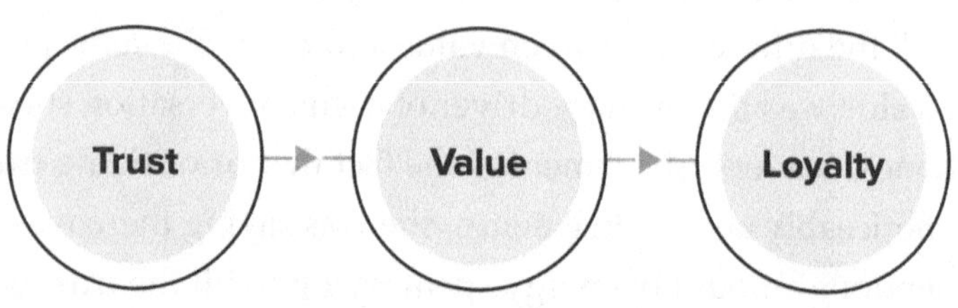

Trust, then value, then loyalty.

NOT

Value, then loyalty, then trust.

If loyalty is the goal and value is the mediator, then trust is the starting point of the customer experience. Sirdeshmukh, Singh, and Sabol's research shows that it's vital for organizations to consider how trust is being built. And, if trust is not being built, then the value proposition begins to decrease.[3]

When the value proposition begins to decrease, loyalty will be weakened, damaged, or lost. Their research demonstrates why it's not enough to just create the best value proposition in your organization; you must create the very best trust proposition first and foremost. We can then not only apply this reality to customers, but to all stakeholders of an organization, especially employees. In the same way that loyalty is sought after from customers by increasing their value proposition through the strengthening of trust, it's critical to seek employee loyalty, their perceived value of the work they do, and organizational trust.

Let's dive in and get clarity on what a trust proposition is.

A value proposition is focused on *worth*.
A trust proposition is focused on *truth*.

To define the concept of a trust proposition, let's break each word down with help from Webster.

Trust = the firm belief in the truth of something.[4]

+

Proposition = a suggested program or plan of action, especially in a business context.[5]

=

Trust Proposition: A plan of action focused on the firm belief in the truth of something.

If we boil it down even more, we can define trust proposition as ***taking action on truth***.

What if the same level of effort, energy, and strategy that is committed to creating a value proposition (taking action on the *worth* of something) was also committed to creating a trust proposition (taking action on the *truth* of something)? This changes the way we think about trust. A trust proposition is not passive, philosophical, ethereal, squishy, illusive, or optional.

Think about the impact and effect on our lives when we encounter people and organizations who embody their trust proposition.

- A leader who *takes action on truth*
- A middle manager who *takes action on truth*
- A front line employee or individual contributor who *takes action on truth*
- A teacher who *takes action on truth*
- A student who *takes action on truth*
- A team who *takes action on truth*
- A board of directors that *takes action on truth*
- A politician who *takes action on truth*
- A spouse / partner / significant other who *takes action on truth*
- Policies, procedures, programs, and pricing that are the outcome of an organization committed to *taking action on truth*

In the same way that an organization's efforts toward building value for their customers are never neutral, our efforts towards building trust with others are also never neutral. We are constantly in a state of building or breaking down trust, of taking action on the truth of something. We will always be involved in strengthening or weakening our trust proposition. Trustworthy people are deeply committed to fulfilling a trust proposition, regardless of the person they are working with, the decision they are making, the challenge they are facing, or the constraints they are experiencing.

Trust is the cornerstone that supports our every interaction, decision, and aspiration. Just as a foundation underpins a building, our trust proposition serves as the groundwork for everything we do. Whether we're working with colleagues or acting as leaders tackling tough choices, the integrity of our trust proposition is constantly being tested and validated.

Since trust isn't an abstract concept, it has structure and form. So, next, we'll explore the simple, yet incredibly significant framework called the Structure of Trust™. Understanding its components will provide us with a solid blueprint for building a resilient, trust-filled organization and help us close the trust gap.

CHAPTER 6
THE STRUCTURE OF TRUST

Imagine that you want to build the house of your dreams.

You do what every homebuyer should do and hire a homebuilder. You assume they are reputable because they have a sharp-looking website, their trucks have the company name on the doors, and they seem to be asking all the right questions during their initial meeting with you. They share with you that they have built houses in different parts of the region where you live, and they've even shown you pictures of houses that they claim to have built. You firmly believe they are professional enough to deliver on your wishes, and you willingly write the check for a large down payment so that they can get started.

But several weeks into the building process, you start to get nervous. Something doesn't feel right. The communication with the builder has gotten quiet. Based on your initial conversations with the homebuilder, it's becoming evident that the building project is not on the proper timeline. You expected delays in progress, but the building process has obviously stalled out. Things seem unclear and disorganized, and you are not on the same page with your builder.

So, you decide to drive to the house lot during a weekday to check in on the builder and their crew. Your stomach drops when you pull up to the lot and see that raw materials are scattered haphazardly around the construction site, but no real work has been done. You finally realize that this self-proclaimed homebuilder is not nearly as qualified as you thought to complete the job you hired them to do. They haven't done all the necessary work to finalize the blueprints, follow the city codes, or hire the right subcontractors. Your dream for an on-time, on-task house building experience has been shattered, and you have no choice but to hire another builder to pick up the pieces and complete the job.

Hopefully you've never experienced this nightmare home-building scenario. But maybe it's similar to another bait-and-switch dynamic you've dealt with in the past or are dealing with in the present in your workplace.

A newly appointed leader declares that they are going to "build trust" in an organization. They say they have done it in the past, and initially you seem confident in their ability to inspire and equip a team. You believe their stories because you so desperately want to reach the end goal: a healthy work culture where every team member is aligned.

But after several weeks, the hope promised during the honey-moon phase of this leader's tenure has become a distant memory. The anticipation of strengthening trust has turned into anxiety, as the organizational culture has settled back into the status quo of terminal toxicity. After speaking with the leader and asking several pointed questions, it's evident that they were only giving lip service to their ability to build trust with their teams. The true reality of employee trust has not been measured or defined. No *real* work is being done. This self-proclaimed "trust builder" has no focus, no buy-in from their team, and no blueprint for trust-building success. Your dream for a healthy workplace culture is shattered, and you are left with only two choices: wait for the current leader to leave, or leave the organization yourself.

Unfortunately, it's probably a safe assumption that you have experienced a workplace dynamic where the promises of leaders to strengthen organizational culture did not ultimately match the final outcome. Good intentions turn into poor delivery. What was touted as an organizational priority falls hard from any semblance of reality. The trust gap widens, and employees show up to work everyday like actors in a play. They check their reality at the door, take on the role of a character, step onto their workplace stage for forty hours a week, and recite their lines to make the director and audience happy. Sameness reigns.

In order to build something great, there must be a well thought-out plan, a blueprint to clarify expectations, and people deeply committed to the discipline and priority of daily carrying out those plans.

The Empire State Building took 7 million human hours to build. It still proudly stands as a central feature of New York City, recognizable from miles away. But imagine if its construction occurred with hundreds of different blueprint versions. Or, worse yet, imagine those 7 million human hours being directed without any blueprints at all. It would have been absolute chaos, and it would never have been completed. The structure of the building is only as good as the structure of the plan and the resolve of the organization to follow that plan.

According to a report from PwC, 'trust' means something different to executives and their workers. All too often, the trust gap is a result of different understandings of what breaks trust: 50% of consumers and 54% of employees report experiencing a trust-damaging event, compared to only 20% of executives. PwC's recent report found that this is because they don't agree on what a trust-damaging event is. Executives define it as something that makes the headlines—15% say security was a trust-damaging issue, and 11% cite legal and compliance issues. However, 36% of consumers point to bad experiences with customer service, causing 63% of these consumers to walk away from a company. Meanwhile, 33% of employees report experiencing bias or mistreatment, and over half of them left their company, saying they no longer trusted it.[1]

In the last chapter we established that trust is the firm belief in the truth of something. We've compared trust (truth) to value (worth) and considered the difference between a value proposition (taking action on worth) and a trust proposition (taking action on truth).

An agreed-upon definition helps us understand and articulate what trust is. A system, process, or framework allows us to live that definition out. It's one thing to have a goal of being more trustworthy, but in order to become a trustworthy organization, you need a *systematic approach*. A system allows something to move from an individual commitment to the identity of an entire company. James Clear, in his wonderful book titled *Atomic Habits* (which I highly recommend), speaks about the importance of systems over goals. "Goals can provide direction and even push you forward in the short term, but eventually a well designed system will always win. Having a system is what matters. Committing to the process is what makes the difference."[2]

In their commitment to better understanding what drives customer value and loyalty, Deepak Sirdeshmukh, Jagdip Singh, and Barry Sabol utilized their research to identify trust-building factors.[3] I've taken their work, expanded upon their research, and developed an organizational and leadership framework called The Structure of Trust™. The Structure of Trust™ enables leaders, teams, and all employees to not only have a shared definition but also a system by which an organization can take action on trust. Put differently, the *Structure of Trust™ enables organizations to live out their Trust Proposition*. The Structure of Trust™ consists of three building blocks and is experienced in two organizational realms.

We will introduce each of the 5 components in this chapter and then do a deeper dive into each in the subsequent chapters.

BUILDING BLOCK OF COMPETENCY

According to the Project Management Institute, competency can be defined as an individual's or an organization's knowledge, skills, attitudes, and behaviors that are causally related to superior job performance. Highly competent individuals or organizations have the ability to perform activities to the levels that meet or exceed performance expectations.[4]

There are many types of competencies required in the workplace: technical competency, leadership competency, management competency, financial competency, time management competency, communication competency, creative competency, risk management competency, sales and marketing competency, customer service competency, and, of course, technology competency.

BUILDING BLOCK OF PROBLEM SOLVING

The American Psychological Association's dictionary of psychology says problem-solving is "the process by which individuals attempt to overcome difficulties to achieve plans that move them from a starting situation to a desired goal, or reach conclusions to the use of higher mental functions, such as reasoning and creative thinking."[5] This is a robust definition of problem-solving that can be boiled down to identifying issues and then overcoming those issues.

BUILDING BLOCK OF CARE FOR OTHERS

Caring for others can be defined simply as the disposition to do good. It's not merely doing good for your own benefit, but also for the benefit of others. Caring for others is about looking out for the needs of others and continually prioritizing their well-being, even if it means that you have to sacrifice something. Caring for others involves empathy, sympathy, emotional intelligence, and compassion.

TRUSTWORTHY PEOPLE

The people of an organization are constantly interacting in various ways, either individually or collaboratively. Whether on a team or cross-functionally, people must be trustworthy in order for the organization to improve its internal and external value, resulting in deepening loyalty.

There is no company culture without people. People are the most valuable resource an organization has. An organization's human resources are the fuel that enables everything that happens in that organization, including organizational culture. Gallup says it well:

> Some leaders mistakenly discount the importance of company culture, no doubt harming business performance. Culture is the unique way that your organization lives out its company purpose and delivers on its brand promise to customers. For this reason, a strong corporate culture functions as a differentiator in the marketplace. It is the special way you attract customers, retain them and turn them into brand advocates. It's also the way you attract highly talented employees and turn them into brand ambassadors. Employees and teams who most align with their company culture consistently perform higher on internal performance metrics than those who least align.[6]

TRUSTWORTHY POLICIES AND PRACTICES

There are written policies that you might find in an employee manual, and then there are the unwritten practices of the organization. For example, what time do people show up at work? How are they interacting at lunch? How are they representing the organization outside the workplace? Do meetings start on time, or are people chronically late? Here's what the company PowerDMS has to say about the importance of policies and procedures in the workplace:

> Policies and procedures keep operations from devolving into complete chaos. When everyone is following policies and procedures, your organization can run smoothly. Management structures and teams operate as they're meant to. And mistakes and hiccups in processes can be quickly identified and addressed. When your staff is following policies and procedures, your organization will use time and resources more efficiently. You'll be able to grow and achieve your goals as an organization. Consistency in practices is also right for employees individually. They know what they're responsible for, what's expected of them, and what they can expect from their supervisors and coworkers. This frees them up to do their jobs with confidence and excellence.[7]

If you are anything like me, a framework in visual form is far more memorable than the principles of that framework being described in written form. Images stick in our minds and make their way to the backs of napkins during mid-morning coffee meetings. They show up on marker boards in conference rooms when teams are wrestling through challenging workplace dynamics. They guide us during complex one-on-one conversations when you are trying to provide feedback consistently among your team members.

Here's the Structure of Trust™ framework in image form.

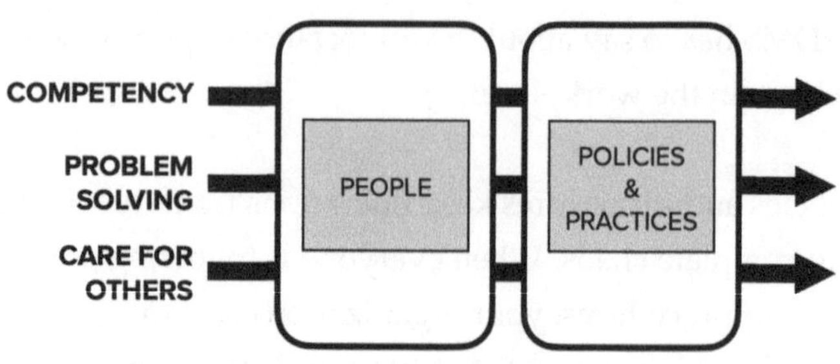

One very important thing to note about the building blocks in the Structure of Trust™: you cannot overcompensate with one building block of trust in order to make up for a deficiency in another building block. In other words, someone may be a competent person in the technical aspects of their job, but if they do not have the ability to identify and solve problems effectively, they will breach trust with others. Similarly, a coworker may be a bulldog when it comes to solving problems. But if they are a bulldog and a bulldozer—someone who minimizes the importance of caring for the needs of others—they will ultimately break down trust.

Ty Cobb, who played twenty-four seasons of Major League Baseball, still holds the record for highest career batting average. His .366 batting average means that for his 11,140 career at bats, he hit safely over one-third of the time! Ty Cobb was enshrined in the Major League Baseball's Hall of Fame in 1936, and his career batting average record may never be broken. But when it comes to building trust within an organization, only operating with one-third of the building blocks won't land you in the Workplace Hall of Fame.

Showing up to work with *only* competency or *only* problem-solving or *only* care for others will render you ineffective at building trust, reduce your value to your organization, result in low levels of loyalty from your coworkers and the customers you serve, and ultimately widen the trust gap.

A building without a solid structure is weak, unsustainable, unpredictable, short-lived, and harmful. Similarly, a workplace culture without a clear and strong trust structure will lead to an organization that is weak, unsustainable, unpredictable, short-lived, and harmful for employees. If given the option of one hundred different versions of trust compared to one that is proven to strengthen trust, increase value, and deepen loyalty, the choice is obvious. The Structure of Trust™ framework allows you to close the trust gap by confidently approaching complex policies and challenging people in a simple, clear, and less emotional way. You have the ability to make trust tangible and disrupt the status quo of organizational distrust.

CHAPTER 7
BUILDING BLOCK OF TRUST #1: COMPETENCY

Major League Baseball umpires are rarely called "competent" by fans—especially by fans of the losing team. Normally, there are a few other choice words, often with juicy adjectives thrown like fastballs from the seats towards the masked villains behind the plate.

But on October 29, 2022, once the last pitch closed out the second World Series game between the Philadelphia Phillies and the Houston Astros, there was no room for criticism. The umpire calling the game that night was veteran Pat Hoberg, and he accomplished something that had never been done before in recorded baseball history: he called a perfect game.

For a player to achieve a perfect game, "a team must not allow any opposing player to reach base by any means: no hits, walks, hit batsmen, uncaught third strikes, catcher's or fielder's interference, or fielding errors which allow a batter to reach base."[1] There have only been a total of 24 perfect games in the hundreds of thousands of Major League Baseball games since 1880.[2]

For an umpire to achieve a perfect game, every pitch must be called correctly. Every current Major League Baseball game uses pitch track technology as a way to capture all of the calls for balls and strikes, so that a thorough post-game evaluation can be done for each umpire in order to develop their skills for future games. Pat Hoberg's umpire scorecard for that World Series game was spotless:[3]

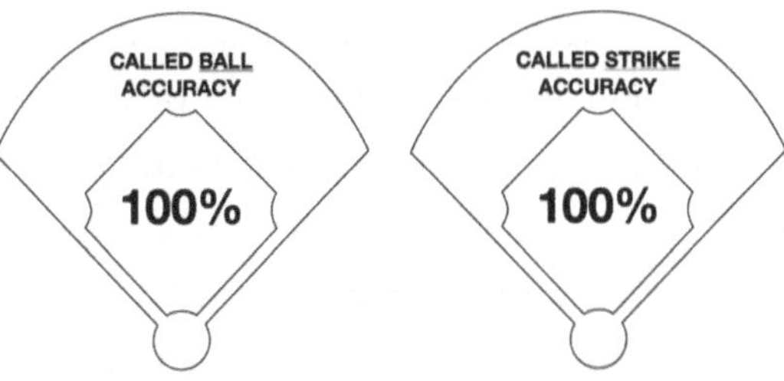

What home plate umpire Pat Hoberg did that late October evening is an outstanding example of workplace competency. Hoberg's years of pitch-after-pitch experience, coupled with ongoing training and feedback, has elevated him to being considered one of the best umpires to ever step behind the plate.

The Office of Human Resources at the National Institute of Health defines competency as:

> …the knowledge, skills, abilities, and behaviors that contribute to individual and organizational performance. Knowledge is information developed or learned through experience, study or investigation. Skill is the result of

> repeatedly applying knowledge or ability. Ability is an innate potential to perform mental and physical actions or tasks. Behavior is the observable reaction of an individual to a certain situation. The target proficiency level for each competency will vary based on an individual's position and the organization's needs.[4]

In my research for this book, I was fortunate to come across a Harvard Business Review article that was written in 1990. Although many of the examples and business cases used are outdated, the core principles of the article are more relevant than ever. In the article, C.K. Prahalad and Gary Hamel assert that an organization will cease to be competitive if the people and practices of the organization are not competent. They use a tree structure to visualize the importance of competence, with competence being the root and the end products being the fruit made available to the customer. No competence roots means no performance fruit.[5]

We know from the Structure of Trust™ that competence is one of three critical building blocks required to close the trust gap.

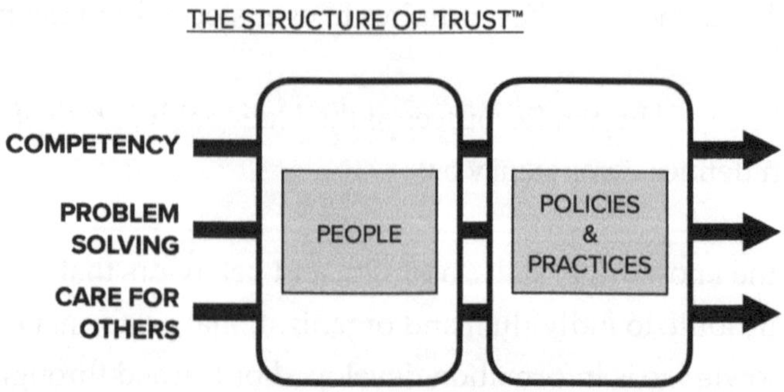

THE STRUCTURE OF TRUST™

Organizations that hire and put up with a culture of incompetence will breach trust, decrease the value they provide, and ultimately lose loyalty. Competencies range in nature from technical to non-technical and from hyper-specific to more general. Technical competencies are specific to a certain job and often require certification, schooling, or extensive on-the-job training. Trust can be instantly broken if a professional hired to do a specific thing in a specific way does not carry out their technical competencies. Airline pilots, dentists, surgeons, pharmacists, car mechanics, architects, and engineers are just a few examples of the countless professions that have very specific competency requirements that, if not consistently carried out, will cause damage to the organization and possible harm to people. Technical competency requirements are usually prominently listed on job postings, resumes, and annual reviews. Non-technical competencies span across various job types, and although they are sometimes less quantifiable, they are equally important. Non-technical competencies are things like time management, conflict resolution, communication, innovation, creativity, teamwork skills, situational awareness skills, and, of course, leadership skills.

Both technical and non-technical competencies are about more than just getting the job done right. They are also vital for building trust. When people and practices in an organization are competency-poor, the long lasting effect will be damaging for both internal employees and external stakeholders, causing the trust gap to widen.

When Kurt Bartolich (CEO of BrandCertain) and I co-authored the *National Survey on Brand and Trust*, we set out to understand the practical and tactical reasons why trust is built up or broken down within each of the building blocks of trust. In this chapter and the next two chapters, I'll provide some key takeaways from the survey for each of the three building blocks of trust.

One of our questions for survey participants was, *"Overall, how would you rate your leaders when it comes to expertise/knowledge?"* We then dug deep into the competency question responses for those who rated their leaders as excellent or good, and also for responses reflecting those who rated their leaders as average, below average, or poor. Here's what we found:

Survey question: *"Why do you feel your leaders are excellent or good at expertise/knowledge?"*

Participants were invited to select all relevant attributes. Here are the ranked responses from employees for why they had a high level of trust for their leaders, specifically for the competency building block of trust:

- Employees are good at what they do: 50%
- Leaders are good at what they do: 43%
- Employees consistently use their skills: 42%
- Employees are efficient at completing their tasks: 41%
- Employees consistently fulfill their responsibilities: 40%
- Employees have a high ability and aptitude to complete a task: 39%
- Usually have the right people in the right places doing the right things: 38%
- Employees consistently implement their training: 32%
- Leaders are subject matter experts: 28%
- Have subject matter experts throughout the organization: 28%

- Our learned experiences help us carry out tasks effectively/efficiently: 26%
- Typically practice before implementing something new: 20%

One of the things I find especially interesting about the responses to this question is that employee trust is influenced *more* by fellow employees being good at what they do than by leaders being good at what they do. Both are very important, but employees more readily call out a trust gap when fellow employees are not capable of competently carrying out their tasks. When other employees have low competency, trust for the leaders is directly affected. The implication for leaders is significant: leadership development for leaders is important, but technical and non-technical competency development for all employees is vital for closing the trust gap.

We then focused on employees who had a low level of trust in the competency of their leaders and asked the following: *"Why do you feel your leaders are average, below average, or poor at expertise/knowledge?"* We provided a list of reasons and asked them to select all attributes that apply. Here are their ranked responses:

- We don't always have the right people in the right places doing the right things: 47%
- Some employees aren't skilled enough for the tasks at hand: 34%
- Some of the methods we use to complete tasks are the wrong ones: 26%
- We lack technical, educational, or vocational training: 21%

- We don't practice new skills enough before implementing: 21%
- We tend to underperform and underdeliver in our tasks: 17%
- We're not technically qualified to do certain things asked of us: 16%
- We consistently miss the mark and our goals: 15%
- Our lack of skills can create dangerous conditions for employees or customers: 15%
- We have very few if any subject matter experts in our organization: 14%
- We're not legally qualified to do certain things asked of us: 9%

Over twenty years ago, Jim Collins authored a must-read business book titled *Good to Great*. In his book, he asserted that in order for organizations to thrive, they need to have the right people in the right seats on the bus. "Through detailed case studies of 11 companies that went from tracking the market to exceeding it by at least 3x, Collins presents the key factors that separate merely good organizations from great ones—from rare leadership to disciplined thinking to the dogged pursuit of a core mission."[6] Here's a compelling excerpt from Collins' book that fully supports what our findings reveal about matching an employee's competency with the right role in their organization:

> When we began the research project, we expected to find that the first step in taking a company from good to great would be to set a new direction, a new vision and strategy for the company, and then to get people committed and aligned behind that new direction. We

> found something quite the opposite. The executives who ignited the transformations from good to great did not first figure out where to drive the bus and then get people to take it there. No, they first got the right people on the bus (and the wrong people off the bus) and then figured out where to drive it. They said, in essence, 'Look, I don't really know where we should take this bus. But I know this much: If we get the right people on the bus, the right people in the right seats, and the wrong people off the bus, then we'll figure out how to take it someplace great.'[7]

Having the wrong people in the wrong seats on the bus is by far the number one way for leaders to ensure a widening of the trust gap related to the building block of competency. But as with any investment of time, money, and people, there are challenges to create a workplace culture where ongoing competency development is the norm, rather than the exception.

So, what's a leader to do? Knowing now that skill-building is not just a nice-to-have but a must-have, how can you ensure that you are closing the trust gap that may be caused by low levels of competency in your organization? Here are four practical steps you can take action on to strengthen the building block of competency with your team:

Step 1

Determine your core competency requirements for every position in your organization. This is not only an HR function, this is a trust-strengthening requirement for every leader in the organization to invest time and energy in. Begin by auditing and updating job descriptions. If you're not utilizing job descriptions to strategically and consistently communicate the competency expectations for team members, you're missing out on low-hanging fruit you can capitalize on right away. A job description needs to be a core working document that is a centering tool for both leader and employee.

Step 2

Define the current condition of your competency reality by assessing gaps between the competencies required for the roles in your organization and the people assigned to carry out those roles. Do you have the right people in the right positions doing the right things in the right way? If so, continue the momentum by elevating this as a top priority with your team. If not, begin now by addressing the gaps with your leaders and build a 6-month plan to move the needle from high levels of concern to high levels of competency. Put as much energy and focus into this competency-building plan as you would for any other type of strategic planning process.

Step 3

Develop a competency framework and share it openly and with regularity. There is no one-size-fits-all template for this. The Chartered Institute for Personnel Development provides guidance on what should be included when developing a competency framework:

> In designing a competency framework, care should be taken to include only measurable components. It's important to restrict the number and complexity of

competencies, typically aiming for no more than twelve for any particular role (preferably fewer), and arranging them into clusters to make the framework more accessible for users. The framework should contain definitions and/or examples of each competency, particularly where it deals with different levels of performance for each of the expected behaviors. It should also outline the negative indicators for that competency—the behaviors deemed unacceptable.[8]

Step 4

Deliver actionable feedback about employee competencies during formal and informal evaluations. Providing a clear evaluation with a proposed plan of action and the resources necessary for building competencies should be an ongoing dialogue, not just a topic of conversation when an employee is underperforming. Actionable feedback for an employee is like an ever-building manifesto intended to help them succeed. Imagine every team member in your organization receiving actionable micro and macro generative feedback fully intended to help them thrive in their work. The cumulative effect for the individual, team, and organization would lead to remarkable results. Being consistent in your expectations with leaders and teams, along with providing them ongoing opportunities to strengthen competencies, is one of the most important things a leader can do to support the employees they are leading.

My wife and I once experienced the benefit of competent leaders in a vivid and unforgettable way. We were flying home after a long weekend in Florida. Before we took off, the pilot announced that high winds were expected and, therefore, we could expect a "bumpier than normal" flight.

You could feel the collective anxiety rise amongst the passengers. I'm not an overly anxious airline passenger, but heavy turbulence is pretty unsettling. Our landing experience was tense to say the least. The plane rocked up, down, and side to side. The intense cross-winds made it bumpy enough to generate unfamiliar sounds throughout the cabin, like the creaking of the overhead bins and the rattling of supplies in the front and back of the plane's cabin.

At what felt like the last moment, the engines roared, and the plane banked hard upward and to the left. We were back in the air, and not a word was spoken by a passenger or crew member for over three minutes. It was unsettling, spooky, and very stressful.

The captain's reassuring voice finally broke the silence. She said they were working with the air traffic controllers to reset their approach and change runways in order to land in a headwind instead of a crosswind. Her voice was calm and confident, and it was evident that she and her co-pilot were in complete control. This crew was the perfect picture of technical and non-technical competence. Their years of training and expertise helped to land the plane safely, and the 150 passengers on board burst into applause as we pulled up to our gate.

This tumultuous experience could have left passengers less likely to book a flight with this airline again. However, the competence and communication the flight crew demonstrated served to strengthen trust instead. After that experience, stressful as it was, I wouldn't hesitate to fly with them again. Competent people delivering competent practices and adhering to competent policies strengthen trust. But this is not possible unless you have the right people in the right roles doing the right things in the right ways at the right times. You may not be an airline pilot trying to land a plane in terrible crosswinds, but you do have people counting on you—both formally and informally—to be as competent as possible to ensure the job is getting done with excellence, integrity, and professionalism.

But we know from the Structure of Trust™ that competency is just one of the three building blocks in order to close the trust gap. Let's do a deeper dive into the second building block of trust: problem-solving.

CHAPTER 8
BUILDING BLOCK OF TRUST #2: PROBLEM-SOLVING

"Houston, we have a problem."

This is perhaps one of the most infamous sentences uttered in the history of space travel. The statement went mainstream when it was highlighted during the climax of *Apollo 13,* a film about three American astronauts in 1970 who experienced catastrophic equipment failure in their tiny spacecraft, hundreds of thousands of miles away from home. In an instant, their highly anticipated moon landing was completely derailed as nearly every vital mechanical system went haywire.

"Houston, we have a problem" was a desperate cry for help that crackled through the radio headphones of staff stationed at the south Texas NASA Mission Control. They would soon realize that this one sentence was a severe understatement. Their dire situation had no precedent and no playbook. They had no plan and no promise of ever setting foot back on earth. As they hurtled through cold space, the dark and uncertain situation they found themselves in was undoubtedly intense.

The team at Mission Control dropped everything to focus their full attention on identifying and solving this very serious problem. They had no other choice but to think quickly and creatively about this problem, moving from a by-the-book sequence of meticulously outlined steps to something that was completely customized and downright off-the-wall.

It was the only way to ensure their colleagues would make it home safely.

Spencer Gardner, the flight activity officer that fateful day, said:

> The most stressful time for me was when I first walked into mission control [with all] that was going on and nobody really knew what the heck was happening for sure. But when you start working the problem and pull things together, it becomes less and less stressful because you're now concentrating on the problem. We were trained to deal with that pressure and stress and concentrate on working the problem that was presented.[1]

The result of Mission Control's efforts was nothing short of miraculous. The solution they provided, coupled with the bravery of the astronauts, resulted in a safe passage home. Their dramatic spacecraft splashdown was shown on television screens in homes around the country.

The problems you and your organization are facing may not be as dramatic as bringing astronauts home from beyond the dark side of the moon. The saga of your people and your practices short-circuiting or failing altogether probably—hopefully—won't become a feature-length film. But your commitment to solving these problems is no less significant for the teams you lead and the organizations you serve. The need to solve the problem, regardless of the scale, is the same.

Spencer Gardner's statement bears repeating and is applicable in any context: "When you start working the problem and pull things together, it becomes less and less stressful because you're now concentrating on the problem." Problem-solving is the second building block of trust, and it's one that is continually tested in light of the increasingly complex workplace realities that every industry is facing. The massive volume of decisions made by so many people every single day dramatically increases the opportunity to solve problems.

THE STRUCTURE OF TRUST™

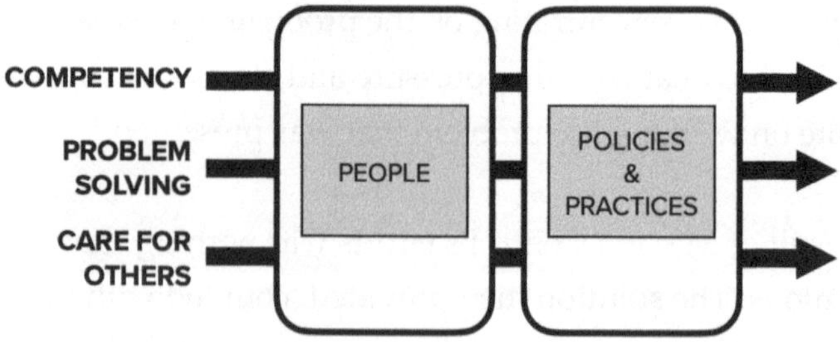

COMPETENCY
PROBLEM SOLVING
CARE FOR OTHERS
PEOPLE
POLICIES & PRACTICES

The American Psychological Association's *Dictionary of Psychology* defines problem-solving as "the process by which individuals attempt to overcome difficulties, achieve plans that move them from a starting situation to a desired goal, or reach conclusions through the use of higher mental functions, such as reasoning and creative thinking."[2]

When problems aren't solved, they can stack up like a sloppy game of Tetris. As the problems stack up without alignment, a fragmented, disorganized, anxiety-inducing reality can quickly derail the focus and productivity of the organization. Some problems go completely unnoticed, while others grow to become "the elephant in the room"—the type that regularly show up in meetings and are evident in policy decisions, product development, program implementation, and hiring. It's frightening to consider how the trajectory of an organization can be so dramatically affected over the long-term as a result of not tending to the problem-solving building block of trust.

The more the problem-solving building block crumbles, the wider the ensuing trust gap becomes. As the trust gap grows more vast, an increasing number of employees begin to feel unable to help move the organization forward. Imagine a rickety suspension bridge high above a canyon that has frayed rope, rotten wood, and is swinging wildly back and forth. Now imagine your employees and customers on this bridge, holding on for dear life as they struggle to keep their balance. Each unresolved problem leads to more problems. As the trust gap widens, the bridge is stretched to its limit.

> Bad decisions can often be traced back to the way the decisions were made—the alternatives were not clearly defined, the right information was not collected, the costs and benefits were not accurately weighed. But sometimes the fault lies not in the decision-making process, but rather in the mind of the decision maker.

> The way the human brain works can sabotage the choices we make.[3]

This observation was first published in an article written by John Hammond, Ralph Keeney, and Howard Raiffa. In their article titled "The Hidden Traps in Decision Making," the authors examined eight psychological traps that can affect the way we make business decisions. My encouragement to you is to read S-L-O-W-L-Y through the following list and reflect on how these eight psychological traps can reduce your ability to strengthen trust through problem-solving:

1. The **anchoring trap** leads us to give disproportionate weight to the first information we receive.
2. The **status quo trap** biases us toward maintaining the current situation, even when better alternatives exist.
3. The **sunk-cost trap** inclines us to perpetuate the mistakes of the past.
4. The **confirming-evidence trap** leads us to seek out information supporting an existing predilection and to discount opposing information.
5. The **framing trap** occurs when we misstate a problem, undermining the entire decision-making process.
6. The **overconfidence trap** makes us overestimate the accuracy of our forecasts.
7. The **prudence trap** leads us to be overcautious when we make estimates about uncertain events.
8. The **recall-ability** trap prompts us to give undue weight to recent, dramatic events.

The authors of this article encourage leaders and teams to avoid these traps by starting with self-awareness:

> The best protection against all psychological traps—in isolation or in combination—is awareness. Even if you can't eradicate the distortions ingrained into the way your mind works, *you can build tests and disciplines into your decision-making process that can uncover errors in thinking before they become errors in judgment.* And taking action to understand and avoid psychological traps can have the added benefit of increasing your confidence in the choices you make.[4]

Read back through the eight psychological traps in decision-making listed above and identify the top three traps your organization consistently struggles with. When do those traps most often arise? How do they affect your team's morale, productivity, attitude, and behavior? How long have you been struggling with these problem-solving traps? If you were able to avoid these traps, caused by the trust gap, what would be different for your organization? What are the conversations you need to have and practices you need to change in order to move these problems from "stuck" to "unstuck"?

Let's consider what the data from the *National Survey on Brand and Trust* revealed as it relates to how trust is built or broken during problem-solving. As was true with the competency building block of trust, we found the data in this case to be many things. Primarily, it was compelling and concerning, eye-opening but instructive.

We encouraged survey participants to choose all options that applied to their experiences. Here were their responses, ranked in order from top to bottom.

Survey question: *"Why do you feel leaders are excellent or good at solving organizational problems?"*

- Open to change: 43%
- Flexible and able to adapt as needed: 43%
- Overall commitment to solving problems: 43%
- Good at managing crisis: 41%
- Willingness to collaborate with others to identify and solve problems: 40%
- Approach problems with critical thinking: 38%
- Have an open door policy and encourage employees to speak up: 38%
- Provide good training: 38%
- Address problems immediately: 37%
- Problems are approached with optimism and as an opportunity to improve: 37%
- Willingness to dig into root causes of problems: 37%

The data conclusively proves that problem-solving leaders and organizations are relentless about following a *process*. Problem-solving can't be comprehensive when under the influence of strong personalities, selfish political agendas, or egocentric power plays. Problem-solving results from a clear, consistent, and disciplined process. And part of that process is a willingness to change.

It should be liberating to know that being open to change for the sake of solving problems builds trust in and of itself. There is zero risk for you to commit to being open to change. Conversely, a leader could choose to weaponize their closed-mindedness and become standoffish at the hint of any request for change. They may feel threatened by others who want to change the status quo.

This damaging dynamic is fueled by insecurity. When this happens over the long-term, the trust gap can feel like an uncrossable chasm. Bosses who are stalwarts to change are psychological bullies who are putting their organization at risk by taking a sledgehammer to the problem-solving building block of trust.

We dug deeper into survey respondents who indicated they had a low level of trust in their leaders. We wanted to discover the attributes and behaviors of leaders causing a gap in trust.

Survey question: *"Why do you feel your leaders are average, below average, or poor at solving organizational problems?"*

- They don't seem to understand why something is a problem: 34%
- Are comfortable with the status quo or set in their ways: 34%
- They put off addressing problems immediately: 33%
- Not good at figuring out the root cause of a problem: 29%
- Employees are overworked: 29%
- Little or no commitment to solving problems: 28%
- Don't provide enough training: 27%
- Don't often understand why a change should be made: 25%
- Not flexible and able to adapt as needed: 21%

Our company has developed a survey instrument called the TrustCentric Organizational Trust Assessment©. This is an important part of the process we use with our clients to help them define reality in a clear and objective way. The goal is to empower them to more readily implement the Structure of Trust™ and develop a blueprint for strengthening organizational trust.

To learn more about the assessment, visit: TrustCentricConsulting.com/Assessment

One of the things we have consistently noticed in the results from this assessment is that the trust-damaging attribute of "employees are overworked" is often rated the lowest of the 49 data points we evaluate. When constant busyness at work, whether real or perceived, interferes with meeting work obligations in a timely manner, it presents both a challenge and an opportunity. The workday is full of problems to solve, and high-trust leaders build trust when they are open to change, able to adapt as needed, and have an overall commitment to solving problems. Leaders destroy the problem-solving building block of trust when they don't seem to understand why something is a problem and when they keep too tight a grip on the status quo.

Justin Ricklefs, Founder and CEO of Guild Collective—who also wrote the foreword to this book—shared with me what he wished he would have learned in his 20s about problem-solving:

He categorizes problem-solving into five different skill levels:

1. **No Skill, Chief Mess-Maker:** This causes a lot of problems. At this level, the person is unaware of the problems they create, and they drain value.
2. **Entry-Level Skill, Chief Finger-Pointer:** They see a problem and complain about the problem. This person doesn't have any ideas about the solution, and waits for someone else to fix it.
3. **Attakid-Level Skill, Chief Team Player:** They see a problem and recommend a solution. This person takes responsibility and sees it through.
4. **Graduate-Level Skill, Chief Responsibility Officer:** They see lots of problems and identify root causes of symptoms presenting themselves as problems. This person takes responsibility for the system and leads others through the changes.
5. **Guide-Level Skill, Chief Sherpa:** They anticipate problems before they happen. They tend to the emotions of those able to lead from a strong, secure, proactive place.

There's a tremendous opportunity for individuals and teams to close the trust gap caused by a lack of problem-solving. Our research shows that *only 32% of leaders were rated as "excellent" in demonstrating problem-solving*.

Do you consider yourself a top problem-solver in the work that you do? Are you at a "guide" level of problem-solving? If not, *why not?* Is problem-solving something that your company struggles with, or are you anticipating problems before they occur? Maybe you're currently experiencing significant growth in your organization and, as you grow, new problems are emerging. This can make it more difficult to follow a sound problem-solving process. What are some of the current problems in your organization that you feel need to be addressed sooner rather than later? What are the warning signs and the root causes moving these problems to the top of your priority list?

During my doctoral program, our cohort spent an entire semester challenging our fellow classmates with what our instructor called a "wicked problem." A "normal" problem is like an onion: you have to peel back the layers in order to resolve the issue effectively.

However, when you peel back the layer of "wicked problem" onion, you find yourself with ten more onions to peel. Complex problems require proven methods to solve them. One such proven method is called Appreciative Inquiry.

According to an article from Benedictine University:

> Appreciative Inquiry draws from the fields of psychology, leadership, and organizational behavior to create a methodology that is nimble and effective. Appreciative Inquiry is based on the principle that organizations are networks of people. When people begin to talk with one another, they co-construct the structures, strategies, and processes they need to move forward.[5]

When faced with a problem, I have found these six Appreciative Inquiry questions to be a helpful guide for beginning the process of closing the trust gap:

1. What led me here?
2. What is the high point of the past?
3. What do I value?
4. What is changing?
5. What's the best future I can imagine?
6. What will it take to get us there?[6]

Problems are unavoidable. *Work is called "work" for a reason.* It takes effort to navigate the complexities and problems that accompany people-related and policy-related issues. Problem-solving is a vital building block that helps close the trust gap. A deep dive into the Appreciative Inquiry model can help guide you through the problem-solving process in a new way.

Regardless of the strategic approach to solving problems you prefer, take action. Make a list of the current problems that need to be solved—and don't do it alone. Ask others to help build the list. This is an effective way to get the problems out into the open. And be open to change. Begin by asking Appreciative Inquiry questions. Most importantly, stay true to the process of solving problems, and let your commitment to strengthening trust fuel your efforts.

You can close the trust gap by becoming a more focused and intentional problem-solver. When it comes to trust, the stakes are too high to allow problems to go unsolved.

CHAPTER 9
BUILDING BLOCK OF TRUST #3: CARE FOR OTHERS

In July of 2017, eight-year-old Stephen and his eleven-year-old brother Noah were playing in the ocean at a popular beach in Florida. They had no idea the riptide below the surface was dragging them away from the safety of the beach and their family. By the time their mother realized what was happening, the boys were over a hundred yards out, trapped in the dangerous current. She and several of her family members frantically swam out to rescue the boys, but quickly found themselves also trapped and endangered. The gap between the family and the shore was wide and growing wider.

Without hesitation, a group of eighty strangers, also enjoying the beach that late afternoon, jumped into action. As they scrambled to organize their rescue, they collectively declared aloud that "this family would not die today." Over the course of an hour, the beachgoers linked arms, linked hands, and held tightly to each other, forming a human chain that stretched from the beach all the way out into the ocean. Some of the rescuers were floating in water as deep as fifteen feet, connected only to those next to them.

This wasn't just a physical connection.

It was *trust*.

Eighty individuals with different backgrounds, different beliefs, different vocations, and different stories had united under a single purpose: saving this family. What a beautiful example of what it means to care for the needs of others. Their commitment to a successful rescue far exceeded any individual's fear of also being swept away.

As a result of this effort—a unified vision powered by trust—all nine family members were rescued.

We've looked at the competency and problem-solving building blocks of trust. The third and final building block of trust, caring for others, is typically the most challenging for the organization to embrace. However, it is no less vital than the other two. Our research shows that 68% of leaders are rated as "excellent" or "good" with the competency building block of trust, 60% of leaders are rated as "excellent" or "good" with the problem-solving building block of trust, and *only 52%* of leaders are rated as "excellent" or "good" with the caring for others building block of trust. This is yet another example of how and why the trust gap is so commonly experienced in the workplace.

Caring for others means having the *disposition to do good*.[1] It's the default attitude that must be present when working with, dealing with, navigating through, and learning from your team. In the workplace, there are dangerous currents pulling at people—sometimes to the point of causing significant organizational harm. When this happens, the only way to "rescue" those people is when others with the disposition to do good take action.

That said, this disposition must be active and present long before noticing someone is frantically flailing at sea and unable to return to the safety of the shore.

Imagine you are a supervisor who has hired a well qualified, seemingly excellent candidate for a role at your company. After several weeks on the job, it's evident the new employee has no issues executing the technical aspects of their role. They do not struggle with the time management or project management aspects of their job. In fact, their experience in the industry has been incredibly helpful for improving certain operations.

But despite all of this, the more you interact with this person, the more concerned you become. When speaking with them, you notice they don't make eye contact. They are easily distracted by their phone, and when they speak, their tone is frequently abrasive—sometimes to the point of being rude. They have an all-business intensity about them that borders on being a bulldog.

Their email responses are snippy. Text message responses are edgy. They tend to speak over people, and they get easily frustrated with other team members struggling with their tasks. Long-time employees are expressing concern and referring to this person as "impatient," "rude," and even "a jerk."

The more you interact with this new hire who sailed through the interview process and is indeed a technical expert in their field, the more you feel *you* are wasting *his* time.

For all their technical expertise, you begin to regret hiring this person.

Even worse, the trust gap widens with this person and with your team.

This disturbing dynamic causes everyone distress. The new employee's attitude seems to be worsening, but you justify it to yourself because of his competency. Exiting this new hire and embarking on the process of refilling the position is not only daunting because it's a pain to endure—it's also embarrassing. You hired this person, and exiting them would demonstrate that you weren't thorough enough during the interview process. So, you stay silent and justify the turmoil. But as we know now, this only serves to destroy trust and harm the organization you serve.

Unfortunately, this is an all-too-common workplace reality. It isn't unusual to come across employees who demonstrate high levels of competency and strong problem-solving skills while simultaneously demonstrating a very low commitment to caring for others.

We know from the Structure of Trust™ that this dynamic is ultimately not sustainable in achieving a workplace culture of high trust. For a leader or team to reach their true trust potential, two out of three building blocks won't cut it.

All three building blocks must be strong to succeed.

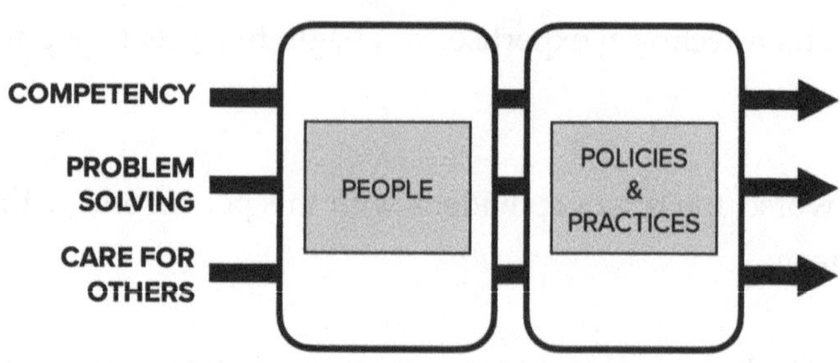

Whether it's with a grumpy employee or jagged-edged policy, the building block of care for others must continue to be strengthened, or else the trust dynamic will be lopsided, unstable, and unsustainable. It's easy to justify why care for others matters. The harder question to answer is *how* to strengthen this building block.

As with the other two building blocks of trust, Kurt Bartolich and I dug deep in the question of *how* with our *National Survey on Brand and Trust*. I hope the specificity and clarity of the data is helpful, hope-giving, and immediately actionable for you.

Survey question: *"Why do you feel leaders are excellent or good at doing acts of kindness/caring for others?"*

- They actively listen: 52%
- Honest and forthright: 46%
- Show compassion towards others: 44%
- Support the needs of the whole person (physical, social, psychological, vocational, spiritual, etc): 42%

- Show patience: 41%
- Remember people's names: 40%
- Calm under pressure: 40%
- Take the time to learn people's stories: 37%
- Serve others without seeking recognition: 36%
- Credit others and not themselves for successes: 34%

Notice what's *not* on the list: Friday office pizza parties, cheap swag, and Employee of the Month recognition or rewards. These antiquated methods are simply not what matters most when an organization or leader commits itself to being intentional about caring for others. If your strategy for demonstrating care for others rests solely on the shoulders of the "fun committee," recognize that the data is clear: the effect will be short-lived, and efforts will ultimately prove to be ineffective.

Now, let's look at and consider the data on the other side of the scale.

Survey question: *"Why do you feel leaders are average, below average, or poor at doing acts of kindness / caring for others?"*

- They don't actively listen: 32%
- Their identities seem wrapped up in their job titles: 28%
- Lack compassion: 27%
- They don't support the needs of the whole person (physical, social, psychological, vocational, spiritual, etc): 27%
- Aren't transparent: 27%
- Don't consistently follow-up: 26%
- Don't take the time to learn people's stories: 26%

- Take credit for successes rather than acknowledging others: 22%
- Aren't honest and forthright: 21%
- Critical and judgmental of others: 20%

I think it's important to consider the damage these percentages represent. A lack of care for others—or what the original researchers of this trust framework described as "operational benevolence"[2]—damages productivity, loyalty, advocacy, and relationships.

The word "benevolence" was expressed in a unique way in an article I read several years ago. The article spoke of a really big elephant named Tim (yes, everybody referred to the elephant by name) who was well-known throughout Kenya. Tim was big in stature, but he was even bigger in heart. The elephant was admired because over the course of his fifty-year life, his gigantic tusks grew to a staggering length and earned him the title "Tusker."[3]

A Tusker is an elephant whose tusks are so long that they scrape the ground. Tim's tusks weighed 100 pounds each. Imagine having 200 pounds of ivory connected to your face and still being lovable. The potential ferocity he could have wielded with his massive tusks was reduced to gentle mischief, which made him all the more lovable. Tim the elephant was revered and loved by all who had the privilege of experiencing his presence because of his consistently kind and gentle demeanor.[4]

The Kenya Wildlife Service said that Tim "was well known and loved throughout Kenya and that he was a benevolent, slow-moving preserver of peace. He was so incredibly intelligent and mischievous, but also a truly gentle giant and in that way a real ambassador for his species."[5] The Kenya Wildlife Service proclaimed Tim as a national treasure, remembered by all who had the privilege to stand in his shadow. What a beautiful picture of what benevolence can do for even the most powerful of giants.

Tim the elephant was not known for his tusks, although they were certainly impressive. Tim was an elephant known for his benevolence *in spite of them*, a trait that inspired people to trust him.

May this story serve as a worthy goal for all of us. Be known as a benevolent, slow-moving preserver of peace, someone who was well-known and loved.

Be an ambassador for our species.

The data overwhelmingly demonstrates that one of the most important ways to be an ambassador who authentically cares for others is by engaging in active listening. Harry Weger defines active listening as "the practice of paying full attention to and absorbing what someone is saying so that the exchange between the listener and speaker is productive and fulfilling. It is an attempt to demonstrate unconditional acceptance and unbiased reflection."[6]

There are many articles, books, online courses, and formal training focused on active listening. Maybe a practical next step for you and your team would be to do a deep dive into the topic of active listening, as it is crucial to understand its benefits and techniques. In the interim, here is a list of nine steps that

Robin Abrahams and Boris Groysberg share in a Harvard Business Review article that will help you get started at becoming a better active listener:

1. Repeat people's last few words back to them.
2. Don't "put it in your own words" unless you need to.
3. Offer nonverbal cues that you're listening—but only if it comes naturally to you.
4. Pay attention to nonverbal cues.
5. Ask more questions than you think you need to.
6. Minimize distractions as much as possible.
7. Acknowledge shortcomings.
8. Don't rehearse your response while the other person is talking.
9. Monitor your emotions.[7]

Imagine every team member in your company approaching every conversion with the intentionality of the steps listed out above. Imagine discussing operational challenges with an ever-increasing commitment to strengthening the building block of care for others through active listening. Imagine being able to close the trust gap by spending zero dollars, and instead just being a better listener.

We don't buy trust. We earn trust. We earn trust one conversation at a time, and every conversation matters.

Andrew Swinand, CEO of the global agency company Leo Burnett, states that:

> Being kind to your employees can help you retain top talent, establish a thriving culture, increase employee engagement, and enhance productivity. When people receive a compliment or words of recognition, it helps them feel more fulfilled, boosts their self-esteem, improves their self-evaluations, and triggers positive emotions. The result: happier, more engaged employees.[8]

Combing back through the data, I've identified other words and phrases that set a high bar for what it means to close the trust gap through this third building block. Pursue the following list of words daily. Affirm when they are present, and be highly sensitive and responsive when the attitudes and behaviors of employees do not reflect them:

> *Honest, forthright, compassion, support, whole person, patience, remembering names, calm, learning people's stories, serving others, crediting others, transparent, consistent, taking time, no judgment.*

Understanding the importance of this building block of trust is critical, and what it requires most of you is intentionality. You don't need a college degree, a new certification, or even years of experience. The heart condition of any organization is deeply influenced by employees who demonstrate that they care for others.

Recall the story of the beachgoers who saved the family at the beginning of this chapter. The power of this building block is almost unparalleled. Care for others can become a powerful catalyst for change in a community of individuals, a group of customers, and even a brand. What can appear to be the simplest form of human decency has the transformative, unifying ability to galvanize people together.

Caring for others should be a constant. It must be lived out and experienced in the policies, practices, and programming your company provides. And it's one of those things that tends to matter a whole lot more than we tend to realize. Elevating our energy and expectation toward caring for others in the same way we do with competency and problem-solving yields powerful, culture-shaping results.

Every day affords you the opportunity to care for others and to move the trust needle from good to better to best.

Take full advantage of each opportunity.

CHAPTER 10
TRUSTWORTHY PEOPLE

"They're not stopping. They're not stopping! *They're not stopping!"*

These were the last words I remember thinking.

A car, going twenty-five miles per hour, failed to yield and struck me while I was riding my bicycle. At the moment of impact, I was knocked unconscious.

I'd been cycling home after a long, full-ironman pre-race training ride. Though my own memories of what happened next are blurry at best, an eyewitness reported the front of the car struck me, then my left shoulder crashed into the windshield. The car continued on another eighty feet while I flipped over the back of the vehicle and flew twenty-five feet through the air like a rag doll. My carbon fiber bike was snapped in half, and I landed on my back.

Hard.

The sound of my impact, glass shattering, and screeching tires alarmed good Samaritans at a nearby neighborhood pool. They ran into the street to help me. Amazingly, one of those people was a critical care nurse named Rolanda. She calmly, confidently, and efficiently stopped the blood that was gushing out of my temple. She also deftly handled the deep cuts in my back caused by the jagged edges of the broken windshield glass. Rolanda—my guardian angel—and the cadre of concerned, helpful people around her stood in the gap and were my lifeline until the paramedics scooped my bloody body off the road.

They were going to rush me to the hospital. The ambulance doors closed with a thump, and they jammed a fourteen-gauge IV needle into my arm to pump a maximum amount of fluids into my severely dehydrated body. The reassuring, skilled paramedic sitting with me kept me stable, alive, and distracted from the trauma.

I would later find out that the paramedics instructed the police at the scene to consider the accident site a crime scene as they were doubtful I would survive.

In my concussed stupor, I repeatedly asked the paramedic the same question over and over: "Has anyone called my wife? If not, her phone number is…" I must have asked a dozen times, unaware that this repetitive cry for help was a symptom of my concussion. One of the few things I do remember during the ambulance ride was the immense relief I felt when I realized I could wiggle my toes and move my feet, as I knew the crash could have easily paralyzed me.

The next thirty minutes were a blur: the lights and sirens, the ambulance ride, the bumpy gurney transport through the sliding glass doors of the ER, and a flurry of medical professionals. They surrounded me, asking questions while pumping me full of meds, running x-rays, CT scans, and preparing me for surgery.

My family arrived soon after, and I could tell by the concerned look on my wife's face and her tone of voice that what had just happened to me was incredibly serious. The surgery to suture up the trauma on the side of my face, left ear, left arm, left hip, and back took five hours and required 300 stitches—a new record for the orthopedic surgeon. I also had three hairline fractures in the transverse process of my spine, which thankfully meant it affected an area that was not weight-bearing. The trauma surgeon later told my wife and me that we needed to buy a lottery ticket because it was a miracle that I survived.

Incredibly, I walked out of the hospital three days later and made a full physical recovery. I suffered no long-term effects besides my scars, which now serve as daily reminders about the gift of life.

My life that day was in the hands of remarkable and trustworthy people, some medically trained and some simply with hearts to help. I was helpless and had no other choice to trust the people around me on that hot, July afternoon. Every single person made a conscious effort to take action to help me. Everyone—from the individual who called my wife to the nurses and doctors that stabilized me in the ER to the surgical team that stitched me back together—demonstrated in a remarkable way every building block of trust: competency, problem-solving, and care for others.

Regardless of what a typical day looks like for you, trustworthy people are vital to achieve results. Whether you save lives, teach children, build bridges, operate machinery, run a small business, mobilize volunteers, conduct research, edit books, design marketing campaigns, manage social media accounts, fly airplanes, work in food service, manage finances, lead large teams, run a nonprofit, or do any other type of job, high levels of trust in people is imperative.

If an organization is achieving all of its goals without a strong work culture, it probably doesn't have the right goals. Further, it probably doesn't have the right goals because it doesn't have the right people making the decisions that matter most. As Ruchi Sinha, researcher and college professor, states:

> In any kind of work environment, you need trust for all kinds of reasons. Without it, you may not feel comfortable bringing your full self to work. You and your teammates may struggle to support one another or openly share ideas and opinions, leading to damaging miscommunications, decreased productivity, and a fear of taking risks that could help you learn and grow in your career.[1]

Outdoor adventure is very important to our family. I've had the privilege of guiding people through thousands of whitewater rafting miles across various rivers. I've also been very fortunate to spend many days hiking and camping in the Colorado backcountry. Whether high up in the mountains or navigating a multi-day river trip in the middle of the Grand Canyon, having an ample supply of clean water is imperative to the well-being of everyone on the trip. After a long day of hiking or rafting, there's a certain temptation to scoop up beautiful-looking water from a nearby bubbling stream and gulp it down. The water is cold, clear, and demonstrates no visible risks that would make you think you might get sick.

But oftentimes, there are imperceptible parasites in that water. They can thrive in even the cleanest looking streams. This tainted water, if not treated correctly or filtered appropriately, can wreak havoc on the body. The water might *look* clean, but in reality, it's often worse than "dirty"—it can be deadly. If you're mindful of the dangers and are disciplined in systematically using the right tools to filter the water (or bring your own), the potential for danger is greatly minimized.

This is analogous to the workplace environment. On the surface, things may look clear and clean. Workplace activity, like water in a high mountain stream, may be moving fast and flowing well. But, *busy activity* doesn't always equal *healthy activity*. In the same way that a backcountry hiker or river runner needs to be hyper-sensitive and diligent in order to trust the health of their drinking water, the leadership of an organization needs to be hyper-sensitive and diligent in order to foster trust among their people.

The responsibility always starts with those in leadership. The leader has to ensure that any potential toxic behaviors or parasites of distrust are filtered out. This is the best way they can start minimizing the danger they otherwise pose to the workplace environment.

Throughout this book, we've learned from the research some of the most common toxins related to the people of an organization that can wreak havoc on a workplace culture. We can boil it down to what I call **The Seven Deadly Sins of Distrust**.

Sin #1: Misalignment of People, Place, and Purpose

The challenge and opportunity of every organization is to ensure trustworthy people are properly placed in roles and given responsibilities to both advance the mission of the organization and ensure the well-being of the workplace community. Every person rowing in the same direction, at the same pace, with the same strength must become the standard, not the exception. Chronic misplacement of people in an organization is ultimately the responsibility of leadership to resolve, not the responsibility of the organization to endure.

You need to have the right people in the right places, doing the right things, in the right way.

Sin #2: Unfit Hiring

The challenge of competency-building, upskilling, or re-skilling won't become easier for leaders and hiring managers anytime soon. Elizabeth Mann Levesque, Instructional Consultant at the University of Michigan, says:

> The nature of work is rapidly changing due to emerging technologies and disruptive forces, such as artificial intelligence, the gig economy, and automation. The exact effect of these and other changes remain unknown, but

> one thing seems certain: the skills that employers value and rely upon are changing.[2]

We will all need to think differently about the actual skills needed to build a team that fuels and fulfills the trust proposition.

You need to hire employees who have the skills to execute the task at hand.

Sin #3: Leaders Blind to Issues

When there are persistent problems in the workplace and the people with the authority to change things are spending their energy fixing things that don't need to be fixed, workplace culture can easily begin to feel unstable and unsafe. This will widen the trust gap and incapacitate an organization's ability to foster psychological safety. According to Stanford professor and researcher Laura Delizonna, "Studies show that psychological safety allows for taking moderate risks, speaking your mind, being creative, and sticking your neck out without fear of having it cut off—just the types of behavior that lead to market breakthroughs."[3]

You need leaders who understand why a problem is a problem.

Sin #4: Embracing the Status Quo

When decisions, initiatives, and resources are allocated because "We've always done it that way," or when the CEO becomes a CE-"NO," you should imagine hazard lights flashing. Justifying suboptimal solutions and resource allocation because "that's just the way it is" isn't a healthy sign. Seth Godin, a brilliant writer and business strategist, provides a helpful list of questions to ask when you sense that decision-makers are needlessly defending the status quo.

"When confronted with a new idea, do you:

- Consider the cost of switching before you consider the benefits?
- Highlight the pain to a few instead of the benefits for the many?
- Exaggerate how good things are now in order to reduce your fear of change?
- Undercut the credibility, authority or experience of people behind the change?
- Grab onto the rare thing that could go wrong instead of amplifying the likely thing that will go right?
- Focus on short-term costs instead of long-term benefits, because the short-term is more vivid for you?
- Fight to retain benefits and status earned only through tenure and longevity?
- Embrace an instinct to accept consistent ongoing costs instead of swallowing a one-time expense?
- Slow implementation and decision making down instead of speeding it up?
- Embrace sunk costs?
- Imagine that your competition is going to be as afraid of change as you are? Even the competition that hasn't entered the market yet and has nothing to lose…
- Emphasize emergency preparation at the expense of a chronic and degenerative condition?

- Compare the best of what you have now with the possible worst of what a change might bring?

Calling it out when you see it might give your team the strength to make a leap."[4]

Your organization and the people in it should *never* be comfortable with the status quo.

Sin #5: Ignoring Feedback

In the conversations I have with leaders—many of them HR professionals—they commonly refer to their employee satisfaction survey as frustrating, unhelpful, counterproductive, and even harmful. Two of the most likely reasons are that the questions aren't the right ones to be asking and / or nothing is being done once the results have been compiled.

The effectiveness of an assessment goes far beyond the deployment of the instrument. The crux of the assessment relies on the organization's response to the results. Moreover, it's crucial that leadership's responses are promptly communicated to those who participated in the assessment. Organizations must be committed to actively listening to the results and either taking action on what has been said or clearly communicating to employees that they have been heard, along with an explanation of why certain feedback is being prioritized. Otherwise, a lack of active listening—or even the *perception* of a lack of active listening—will result in an abundance of active speculation and distrust.

Leaders must be willing to actively listen to formal feedback.

Sin #6: Identity Wrapped Up in Job Titles

When the org chart becomes an ego chart, you can be sure there is a persistent trust gap. Army veteran and business leader Carson Petry sums it up well:

> Unchecked ego is a dangerous and destructive force that can negatively impact both individuals and organizations. At its core, ego is the sense of self-importance that we all possess. While some level of ego is healthy and necessary, an unchecked ego can lead to arrogance, entitlement, and a belief that one is above reproach. When left unchecked, this can lead to toxic leadership.[5]

Middle managers can play a vital role in closing the trust gap and keeping egos in check. In a healthy organization, middle managers understand leadership's vision and direction. They demonstrate this when they clearly and accurately articulate expectations, goals, and accountability to frontline employees carrying out vital, day-to-day work. In a toxic workplace, middle managers often become neutralized as they are neither given the authority to lead nor the respect of those who follow. Middle managers often don't get enough credit, even though their unique position usually exposes them to the truth of how things really are in the workplace culture.

Annual reviews, job promotions, and restructuring are all prime opportunities to ensure that identities and job titles are kept in check, as opposed to being overinflated by ego.

People's identities should not be wrapped up in their job titles.

Sin #7: Terminal Toxicity

When people in positions of authority weaponize distrust, they are setting in motion irreparable interpersonal or organizational harm. The victims of terminal toxicity become traumatized and permanently scarred.

Here's how Laura Delizonna puts it:

> The brain processes a provocation by a boss, competitive coworker, or dismissive subordinate as a life-or-death threat. The amygdala, the alarm bell in the brain, ignites the fight-or-flight response, hijacking higher brain centers. This 'act first, think later' brain structure shuts down perspective and analytical reasoning. Quite literally, just when we need it most, we lose our minds. While that fight-or-flight reaction may save us in life-or-death situations, it handicaps the strategic thinking needed in today's workplace.[6]

Distrust must never be fueled by intention. A person intentionally sowing seeds of distrust should not remain in your organization.

If you recognize any of the sins above, it's time for your organization to take responsibility and make a plan to change.

Start by following this five-step framework, then expand on it and make it your own:

1. **HIRE** competent problem-solvers who are committed to caring for others.
2. **ACQUIRE** insight into your employees' current reality and state of trust by conducting a robust assessment.
3. **INSPIRE** those you lead by being the *first* one to live out the trust proposition.
4. **FIRE** terminally toxic people. Full stop.
5. **RETIRE** the status quo mindset. Give it a set of golf clubs, and tell it goodbye.

Hire, acquire, inspire, fire, and retire. When you do this, you will grow a company full of champions who are relentlessly committed to closing the trust gap.

Don't wait.

CHAPTER 11
TRUSTWORTHY POLICIES AND PRACTICES

In January of 2020, Sonos, a popular, high-end entertainment system speaker manufacturer, faced significant backlash from customers. Older products weren't receiving necessary software upgrades. The CEO, Patrick Spence, took responsibility and sent a letter to all Sonos customers, apologizing and committing to making things right:[1]

A Letter from our CEO: All Sonos products will work past May

> *We heard you. We did not get this right from the start. My apologies for that and I wanted to personally assure you of the path forward:*
>
> *First, rest assured that come May, when we end new software updates for our legacy products, they will continue to work just as they do today. We are not bricking them, we are not forcing them into obsolescence, and we are not taking anything away. Many of you have invested heavily in your Sonos systems, and we intend to honor that investment for as long as possible. While legacy Sonos products won't get new software features, we pledge*

to keep them updated with bug fixes and security patches for as long as possible. If we run into something core to the experience that can't be addressed, we'll work to offer an alternative solution and let you know about any changes you'll see in your experience.

Secondly, we heard you on the issue of legacy products and modern products not being able to coexist in your home. We are working on a way to split your system so that modern products work together and get the latest features, while legacy products work together and remain in their current state. We're finalizing details on this plan and will share more in the coming weeks. While we have a lot of great products and features in the pipeline, we want our customers to upgrade to our latest and greatest products when they're excited by what the new products offer, not because they feel forced to do so. That's the intent of the trade up program we launched for our loyal customers.

Thank you for being a Sonos customer. Thank you for taking the time to give us your feedback. I hope that you'll forgive our misstep, and let us earn back your trust. Without you, Sonos wouldn't exist and we'll work harder than ever to earn your loyalty every single day.

If you have any further questions please don't hesitate to contact us.

Sincerely,

Patrick Spence
CEO, Sonos

Sonos combated bad technological policy and procedure with two things: a good communication policy and a promise to implement technology that would fix the problem. They rectified their mistake, demonstrating competency, problem-solving, and care for others. The company did everything possible to close the trust gap they had created. Jonathan Hemus, Managing Director and crisis management consultant at Insignia Crisis, identified seven things that made this response a masterclass in crisis communication: timeliness, empathy, contrition, the Big "A" (apology), remedial action, humility, and authenticity.[2]

The building blocks of trust apply to the people within an organization, but also to the policies and practices of an organization. Trustworthy practices must also be competent, designed to problem-solve, and must demonstrate care for others. Hiring trustworthy people and expecting them to carry out organizational practices that are devoid of trust will yield suboptimal results at best. Conversely, best-in-class policies and procedures that are stewarded by toxic employees will never lead to the fulfillment of the mission of an organization.

Imagine a hiker lost in the woods, frantically trying to find his way home. He's walking in circles, despite having important, necessary tools—a map and compass—in his backpack. Prior to his hike, this individual had dismissed the notion of receiving orienteering training. So, the tools he has are useless and, as a result, he will continue to flail in the woods.

Now, let's flip the scenario. A hiker with ample orienteering training is otherwise equipped with a broken compass and a map from a completely different region of the mountain range. Despite his excellent map-reading skills, his tools are useless, which hinders his ability to find his way home.

It's easy to underestimate or to take for granted the importance of policies and practices. The company PowerDMS explains:

> Policies and procedures are an essential part of any organization. Together, policies and procedures provide a roadmap for day-to-day operations. They ensure compliance with laws and regulations, give guidance for decision-making, and streamline internal processes.[3]

Policies and practices keep an organization focused and on track, enabling employees to deliver optimal products and services to customers. Gaps in trust will form when the policies and practices of an organization are not competent, do not solve the right problems, and do not demonstrate care for others.

One of the most powerful practices within an organization that builds up or breaks down trust is the way they handle meetings. The frequency, purpose, duration, attendees, content, and action items all matter. Why?

Because meetings gobble up gigantic amounts of time during the workweek.

Brier Cook, Engagement Strategy Advisor for Carleton University, shares:

> In the United States alone, there are around 55 million meetings held each week. Our research shows that people attend an average of between 11 to 15 meetings per week. Of these meetings, the most common types are weekly team meetings and project meetings. Nearly 50% of executives attend between 6 and 15 meetings per week, while managers attend more than 16. Employees at most companies will spend up to 33% of their work-

> week in meetings and organizations as a whole spend around 15% of their time in meetings.[4]

While the right type of meetings are crucial, meetings are always costly. There are direct payroll costs based on the number of people in the room multiplied by their hourly wage.

Here's an eye-opening example: a two-hour meeting with fifteen people in the room who make an average of $75,000 per year has a wage cost of $1,125. Let's say that group meets once every two weeks. The annualized cost of that meeting *alone* is $29,406.

Meetings have other costs, too. Whatever the attendee isn't working on as a result of time spent in the meeting creates an indirect cost. Depending on the role of the employee, these indirect costs could be significant.

One of the most practical ways to identify trust gaps in your organization is by doing an audit of your meetings. Patrick Lencioni, author of the must-read book *Death by Meeting*, says it well:

> Even if people had nothing else to do with their time, the monotony of sitting through an uninspired staff meeting, conference call, or two-day off-site would have to rank right up there with the most painful activities of modern business culture. And when we consider that most of the people struggling through those meetings do indeed have other things to do, that pain is only amplified.[5]

It can be hard to trust a company you feel is wasting your time.

One way to assess if a meeting should even take place is by using a simple flow chart like the one below.[6] Print it off, share it with your team, and honestly assess whether or not your current approach to meetings is competent, problem-solving, and demonstrative of care for others.

If you find your current practice is not representative of all three building blocks of trust, you have two options: you can choose to keep meetings unchanged and feed the status quo monster, or you can change the way you schedule and conduct meetings to align more closely with the building blocks of trust. Always remember the power of eliminating meetings if you find they are destructive or add no real value—sometimes, this may be the most trust-strengthening action you can take.

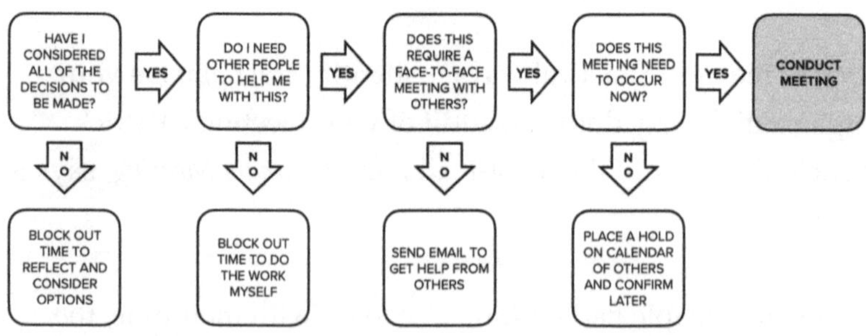

Meetings are just *one* of the areas where trust is built up or broken down within an organization. There are many other types of policies and practices that employees interact with regularly: attendance policies, cell phone policies, health and safety policies, grievance policies, email policies, conflict of interest policies, communication policies, smoking policies, and more. In the same way that employees can be evaluated and held accountable to representing the building blocks of trust, so too should policies, practices, and procedures.

Every organization has the opportunity to shift the role of a policy or practice from "judge and jury" to a trustworthy, strategic opportunity to differentiate the employee and customer experience. It's rare to see companies truly embrace this opportunity, and sometimes the simplest things make a big difference. Here are a couple of examples:

During the peak of COVID-19, every business was reeling, including Major League Baseball. The Pittsburgh Pirates seized this opportunity to exemplify the building blocks of trust and deepen their trust proposition with a fan. Here's an excerpt from an SBNation article that explained their special delivery:

> The fan opened his mail to find a foul ball and a letter from the Pirates, saying the ball landed in his seat during a game played without fans—so it was retrieved and mailed to him as a memento of the 2020 season. Obviously the team didn't need to do this. It wasn't expected. However, they went to the effort not only to get a ball from the stands, but find the seat owner and ensure they felt part of the action, even when they couldn't be at the ballpark. This is what it's all about. Feeling emotionally connected to a team, even when you can't cheer for them in person. The Pirates went above and beyond, and this is awesome. Now the fan will be one of the few people to have a foul ball from the season that was never played in totality.[7]

From jeers to cheers. Here's the letter the season ticket holder received with the foul ball:[8]

Pittsburgh Pirates Baseball Club
PNC Park at North Shore
115 Federal Street Pittsburgh, PA 15212

SURPRISE!!!

During a home game, a foul ball landed in your seat at PNC Park.

Robbie Incmikoski at AT&T SportsNet happened to grab it for you and you'll find it enclosed.

We wish you could have been here in person to make the catch yourself! Hopefully we'll see you back in your seat at PNC Park in 2021.

But until then, enjoy this momento from the 2020 season.

THANK YOU for your consistent support and loyalty to the Pittsburgh Pirates Organization.

Let's go Bucs!!
The Pittsburgh Pirates

When the common practice of an organization is to take the essence of a customer experience and deliver excellence to them in a simple-yet-powerful way, deep wells of trust are formed instead of wide gaps.

Another recent example is one I personally experienced on a flight home from a business trip. It was a Wi-Fi experience gone bad. I was looking to get caught up on several work items and paid $8 to connect to the plane's Wi-Fi. My payment went through, and the connection was established initially, but it stopped working after just a few minutes. After repeated attempts to reconnect, I closed the lid of my laptop and leaned my head back for a high altitude nap. It wasn't the end of the world, but I was a bit frustrated to have paid for something that didn't work and to have wasted a couple of hours of focus to catch up on various items (including the writing of this book).

I thought nothing of the incident once the plane landed, and I carried on with the rest of my day. But to my pleasant surprise, I received the following email a few hours after my trip:

> *Southwest Airlines*
> *SouthwestAirlines@wifi.southwest.com*
>
> *INTERNET REFUND*
>
> *Dear Cory,*
>
> *Our system shows that you may have had a poor connectivity experience onboard your recent flight. We want you to have the best experience possible and apologize for any inconvenience.*
>
> *To make things right, we're refunding your $8 Internet purchase. We look forward to welcoming you on board again soon and providing a better connectivity experience next time!*
>
> *Sincerely,*
> *Your friends at Southwest Airlines*

These are two simple but meaningful examples of how organizations can leverage their policies and practices to move away from just getting by to becoming best-in-class by living out their trust proposition.

If you were to run all of your policies, procedures, and practices through the framework of the Structure of Trust™, what would the results reveal? Would the building blocks be strong in certain areas and weak in other areas? What would each company policy's rating be for competency? For problem-solving? For care for others? Are you listening actively to people who interact most with the policies and practices and understanding their specific concerns? If so, what are you doing with those concerns? If you're not actively listening, what's holding you back from creating a listening and learning initiative? What are the policies and practices stuck in the status quo and in deep need of an overhaul? Are you in need of moving your policies and practices from just getting by to best in class?

Now, not later, is the time to strengthen your trust proposition and close the trust gap within your policies and practices.

CHAPTER 12
TAKING ACTION ON TRUST

"Giant blobs of seaweed are hitting Florida. That's when the real problem begins."

The article headline caught my attention for two reasons.

First, the Florida beaches are a place our family frequently visits, and we have experienced copious blooms of seaweed both in the water and on the beach. Needless to say, the seaweed was not an expected or optimal part of our experience. Second, as someone deeply committed to helping organizations assess and take action on strengthening trust, I think about the effects of trust and distrust constantly.

So, when I read the headline of the article, I felt this disruptive phenomena of sargassum (giant blobs of seaweed) and its highly damaging effect on the nation's pristine beaches is analogous to the highly damaging effects of distrust on leaders, teams, and organizations.

I clicked on the headline and slowly read through the compelling, troubling, and vexing article, wonderfully written by NPR reporter Emily Olson.

Here were some of the sentences that lifted off the page for me:

- "...an influx of algae called sargassum is leaving stinky brown carpets over what was once prime tourist sand."
- "Deciding what to do with it is proving more challenging the more we learn about it…"
- "Sargassum is a type of buoyant, rootless algae that bunches up in islands and floats around the ocean, and the density of that (sargassum) belt's clusters keeps increasing…"
- "Once ashore, sargassum isn't just unsightly or cumbersome to swim around—it stinks. The seaweed starts to decay within twenty-four hours of hitting the shore, releasing hydrogen sulfide and the smell of rotten eggs. There's some evidence to show that those gasses can cause nausea and headaches or aggravate respiratory issues."[1]

I then started reading back through these highlighted quotations from the article, and I reflected on how distrust in the workplace has a very similar origin story and effect on organizations. I translated the key points of the article through the lens of organizational distrust:

- An influx of highly disruptive behaviors and actions is leaving toxic residue all over what was once a healthy organization.

- Deciding how to handle this level of distrust is proving to be more challenging than what leaders and teams expected or were prepared for.
- Distrust is a type of pervasive relational and organizational dynamic that bunches up in formal and informal silos and floats around the company culture. Evidence shows this is a result of low levels of competency, problem-solving, and care for others.
- Once a part of an organization, distrust is not just unsightly—it stinks. There's evidence that shows the effects of distrust can affect an employee's physical, social, psychological, and vocational well-being.

If action isn't taken and collective resources aren't allocated to maintain the healthy condition of our beautiful beaches, an invasive species will do irreparable harm not only to the environment, but also to the economy of that region. In the same way, if action isn't taken and collective resources aren't allocated to maintain the healthy condition of a workplace culture, an invasive species will grow, thrive, and throttle the well-being of an organization. If left unaddressed, the organization may find itself with a stinky, toxic, highly disruptive, costly mess on their hands.

I believe that the best way to *end* this book is to ensure it is a *starting point* for you, the reader. This book represents a new way to think about, articulate, measure, prioritize, and ultimately strengthen trust. Leaders are responsible for ensuring organizational trust stands the test of time.

TAKING ACTION ON TRUST

What you do with what you've read will have long-lasting effects on those you lead. You can start by taking action in the following five ways:

Step 1 - Start with Self-Reflection

The condition of corporate trust begins with the condition of individual trust. We must constantly and proactively take stock of how we are individually showing up in meetings, in hallways and parking lot conversations, on virtual calls, in policy decisions, and in performance reviews.

Donald and Charles Sull conducted a meta analysis of thousands of corporate culture studies. As a result of these studies, they shared that:

> Leadership consistently emerged as the best predictor of toxic culture. The importance of leadership will surprise no one, but it does underscore a fundamental reality: leaders cannot improve corporate culture unless they are willing to hold themselves and their colleagues accountable for toxic behavior.[2]

There's no shortage of questions we can ask ourselves. What are the conditions of the building blocks of trust in my life? How can I become more competent? Am I solving the right problems? Do I have a commitment to solving problems in a way that is collaborative and helpful? Am I truly demonstrating comprehensive care for others? In what specific ways can I improve my active listening skills? Am I appropriately vulnerable and transparent in service to others? Do I need to make amends with a coworker and apologize? Is my identity wrapped up in my job title? What changes do I need to make in the way that I am leading others?

Trust is not something that can be exported, delegated, or farmed out to a third party vendor. Trust begins with you.

Step 2 - Make Trust Essential

Stephen Covey, author of the best selling book *The Speed of Trust*, says, "Trust is essential to well-being."[3] He also provides three poignant challenges, along with their accompanying effects:

1. Take the risk to care because it unlocks human connection.
2. Be deliberate with intentions so you put purpose into action.
3. Strengthen integrity to increase your credibility.[4]

I especially appreciate the effect of making trust essential: it unlocks human connection, puts purpose into action, and increases credibility. A trust proposition means we take action on truth—as individuals, as teams, and as organizations.

Both the data and our lived experiences are clear: there's no way to fully achieve all of our leadership and organizational goals without a strong workplace culture. Real workplace trust is the sum of every individual taking action to strengthen it.

We must prioritize trust because trust is inherently essential. We need to have a heightened sensitivity to toxicity and factors that degrade trust. Your trust radar needs to be continuously monitoring the environment to ensure trust is embraced.

Remember the biohazard symbol discussion back in Chapter Three? The gaps in the circles symbolize toxicity in the system.

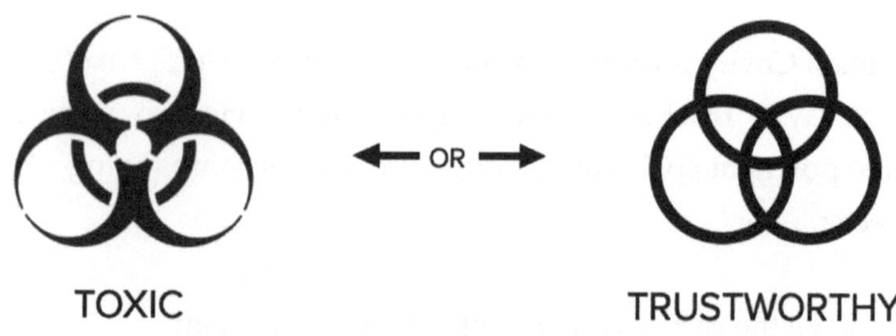

Keeping trust essential will help to ensure your organization stays on the right side of this visual.

Step 3 - Move the Structure of Trust™ from this book to the Back of a Napkin

Some of the most meaningful conversations I've had with leaders have taken place over a cup of coffee alongside the Structure of Trust™ drawn onto the back of a napkin. The framework, originally proven over twenty years ago by three marketing researchers[5], is more relevant and helpful today than ever. There are many lists of trust attributes, behaviors, and tactics. But what I have found most helpful about the Structure of Trust™ is that it's simple enough to be memorable, specific enough to be used as an evaluative tool, and general enough to be applicable for every person and every policy in an organization.

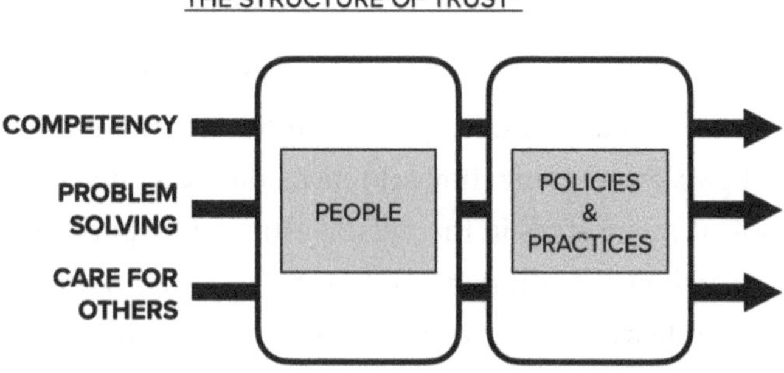

We've discussed the three building blocks of trust: competency, problem-solving, and care for others. Together, they empower and are empowered by two realms: policies and practices. The framework is simple, but not simplistic. The implications of having a consistent framework of trust that easily generates instructional and evaluative opportunities for strengthening trust are both helpful and hope-giving. Move the model from the book to your next weekly staff meeting, one-on-one coaching session, and coffee-meeting napkin conversation.

Step 4 - Begin Assessing Trust

Leadership and management guru Peter Drucker famously said, "What gets measured gets managed."[6] Thankfully, trust *is* something that can be measured and managed.

I hear this frequently: "The last thing we need is another survey to fill out." I get it. I also understand that this stems from a pervasive feeling of cynicism, survey fatigue, and low completion rates for employee satisfaction surveys. And yet, it is crucial to remember that survey fatigue is often because employees *are tired of giving feedback they know leadership will not act upon.*

We've found that a thorough trust assessment with the right questions can yield positive, generative conversations to close the trust gap. An organization and its leadership must do more than look at themselves in the mirror—they must periodically do a comprehensive company "CT Scan" in order to understand more clearly what is causing the symptoms they are experiencing.

Defining reality can induce feelings of shame—but it shouldn't. Instead of it feeling like an indictment, it should be viewed with gratitude: Now you know something you didn't know before.

And *now* you can act on it.

It is and always has been the responsibility of the leader and the organization to prioritize assessments so that blind spots can be discovered and improvements can be made. Assessments, when done correctly, make invisible problems visible, and therefore easier to tackle. Courageous leaders who understand the value and power of trust embrace the opportunity to learn and to move things from invisible to visible.

They know they can make the visible actionable.

To learn more about the assessment, visit:
TrustCentricConsulting.com/Assessment

Step 5 - Develop a Trust Blueprint

The research that Kurt Bartolich and I did for the *National Survey on Brand and Trust* revealed many things about the dismal reality of distrust across all industries. At the same time, it also revealed very helpful, practical, and actionable priorities any leader, team, or organization can focus on in order to close the trust gap.

If a large, blank sheet of blueprint paper was rolled out in front of you, and you were to start developing a plan to close the trust gap in your organization, here are the five things, based on the empirical evidence, that I would encourage you to prioritize over the next six months:

1. Receive regular employee feedback *and do something about it.*
2. Have more honest conversations *and listen more than you speak.*
3. Be deeply committed to increasing transparency *knowing it is appropriate and helpful.*
4. Develop a clear trust strategy *knowing it is a blueprint you can continue to build on.*
5. Create a shared commitment to clear ownership of tasks and projects *and hold yourself and others accountable.*

Ultimately, you always have the choice to take action on trust. As a leader, you are not just responsible for the well-being of your fellow employees today. You have the privilege and opportunity to be responsible for their well-being in perpetuity.

As a leader, you have the power to address the trust gaps in your organization. You can ignore them, justify them, and widen them. Or, you can measure them, name them, lean into them, correct them, *and close them*.

Closing the trust gap requires ongoing effort and attention. It involves discipline and a steady, courageous focus on all three building blocks of trust in every interaction, from one-on-one conversations to weekly meetings to policy reviews, and everything between.

Trust is the firm belief in the truth of something. So, I ask you: *When you show up to work every day, are you fighting for truth in service to others and on behalf of the mission of the organization?*

In reading this book, you've heard the call to action.

And if this book has helped you realize you've struggled to strengthen trust with others, step one is to forgive yourself. Wallowing in failure is not the way forward. We only fail when we stop trying. So even if it takes an act of radical acceptance: forgive. Then, take action to make things right. This book has armed you with a clear model for strengthening organizational trust. You are now much more likely to have a heightened sensitivity to causes of toxicity, and you have taken the first step toward moving yourself and your organization towards a trustworthy future.

If you are an influencer or leader who has the opportunity to help shape workplace culture, let this book serve as a call to action and a reckoning full of empathy and grace. I hope this book has empowered you to take swift, decisive action when you recognize trust gaps in the future.

If you have minimal influence in your current role and reading this book has helped you realize you're in a toxic culture, your call to action may involve eventually exiting the organization.

No matter your specific situation or history, my hope is that, as a result of this book, you feel equipped, energized, inspired, and motivated to take action on trust.

Live out your trust proposition.

You have the power to close the trust gap.

TRUST QUOTES

One of the benefits of doing research for this book was coming across some incredible quotes on trust. Some are included earlier in the book, while others only appear in this list. I wanted to share this great list from some wonderful thought leaders and trust gurus.

> "Contrary to what most people believe, trust is not some soft, illusive quality that you either have or you don't; rather, trust is a pragmatic, tangible, actionable asset that you can create."
>
> STEPHEN COVEY

> "If people like you, they will listen to you. But if people trust you, they will do business with you."
>
> ZIG ZIGLAR

"People follow leaders by choice. Without trust, at best you get compliance."

JESSE LYN STONER

"Trust is the currency for the future."

PENNY AND SARA BOLING

"Trust is knowing that when a team member does push you, they're doing it because they care about the team."

PATRICK LENCIONI

"The best leaders build trust from the inside out. An organization that does not have the trust of its employees can never earn the trust of its customers."

SCOTT BARADELL

"You don't have a remote work issue. You have trust issues."

JUSTIN WRIGHT

"There's no team without trust."

PAUL SANTAGATA

"Without trust, you generate a dysfunctional organization and teams. There is no meaningful connection between a group of people. It's just meaningless coordination. It is trust that shifts a group of people into a team."

MARIE-CLAIRE ROSS

"Leadership ultimately comes down to creating conditions for trust within an organization."

COLIN POWELL

"The problem is not in the absence of knowing what to do, but the absence of doing it."

PETER DRUCKER

"Your words and deeds must match if you expect employees to trust in your leadership."

KEVIN KRUSE

"Most of us consider trust to be built slowly, with verification, and in degrees...trust is created by a combination of things and, while the end result is almost magical, the process cannot be rushed."

MAC RICHARD

"Trust is the glue of life. It's the most essential ingredient in effective communication. It's the foundational principle that holds all relationships."

STEPHEN R. COVEY

"A team is not a group of people who work together. A team is a group of people who trust each other."

SIMON SINEK

"If your actions don't align with your values, your employees won't trust you."

JUSTIN WRIGHT

"The glue that holds business relationships together, that is trust, and this trust is purely based on integrity."

BRIAN TRACY

"When people don't trust each other, everything is slow and takes a million meetings. It's like sludge and they block each other. Nothing moves quickly. You end up doubling up on resources. If you could just trust each other, you could talk about issues."

KATE MORRIS

"Trust is earned when actions meet words."

CHRIS BUTLER

"When people honor each other, there is a trust established that leads to synergy, interdependence, and deep respect. Both parties make decisions and choices based on what is right, what is best, what is valued most highly."

BLAINE LEE PARDOE

"Trust is built with consistency."

LINCOLN CHAFEE

"Trust has to be the highest value in your company, and if it's not, something bad is going to happen to you."

MARC BENIOFF

"If you don't have trust inside your company, then you can't transfer it to your customers."

ROGER STAUBACH

"Trust-and-inspire leadership is not soft, weak, without expectations and accountability. Trust-and-inspire leaders can be authoritative without being authoritarian. You can be decisive without being autocratic. You can be visionary without being exclusive. You can be strong without being forceful. You can be detail oriented without being distrusting. You can have control without being controlling."

STEPHEN COVEY

“It takes twenty years to build a reputation and five minutes to ruin it. If you think about that, you'll do things differently.”

WARREN BUFFETT

“Trust is the highest form of human motivation. It brings out the very best in people.”

STEPHEN R. COVEY

“Trust is built and maintained by many small actions over time.”

LOLLY DASKAL

“Content builds relationships, relationships are built on trust. Trust drives revenue.”

ANDREW DAVIS

“Whoever is careless with the truth in small matters cannot be trusted with important matters.”

ALBERT EINSTEIN

“It is mutual trust, even more than mutual interest, that holds human associations together.”

H. L. MENCKEN

"Every sale has five basic obstacles: no need, no money, no hurry, no desire, no trust."

ZIG ZIGLAR

"Leadership requires five ingredients: brains, energy, determination, trust, and ethics. The key challenges today are in terms of the last two: trust and ethics."

FRED HILMER

"When a gifted team dedicates itself to unselfish trust and combines instinct with boldness and effort, it is ready to climb."

PATANJALI

"Trust is like blood pressure. It's silent, vital to good health, and if abused it can be deadly."

FRANK SONNENBERG

"Don't ever break someone's trust. Once you do, then nobody wants to do business with you."

ROBERT BUDI HARTONO

"Trustful people are pure at heart, as they are moved by the zeal of their own trustworthiness."

CRISS JAMI

"Trust is a perception, and you can measure perceptions through anonymous surveys to see the level of confidence someone may have in a team or a leader. You can benchmark it, track it, and see it move and grow. You can measure the inputs and the overall outcome and quantify it. We tend to value what we can measure, and we work on what we can measure. And the idea that you can measure trust is a big idea. So in that sense, less in the eye of the beholder. Using common criteria, we can see the level of confidence people have in our team and we have in each other."

STEPHEN COVEY

"Earn trust, earn trust, earn trust. Then you can worry about the rest."

SETH GODIN

NOTES

INTRODUCTION

1. Gupta, Shalene. "There's a Trust Gap between Business Leaders, Employees, and Consumers. This Is Why." Fast Company. Fast Company, March 28, 2023. https://www.fastcompany.com/90871322/pwc-study-business-companies-trust-gap.
2. Robinson, B. (2021, September 5). New Study Shows A Lack Of Trust Between Employees And Employers. Forbes. https://www.forbes.com/sites/bryanrobinson/2021/09/05/new-study-shows-a-lack-of-trust-between-employees-and-employers/?sh=794fcdfd395b.
3. McBride, A. (2023, May 12). Only 21% of U.S. Employees Trust The Leadership At Work. The Hill. https://thehill.com/lobbying/4001575-only-21-of-u-s-employees-trust-the-leadership-at-work/.
4. Gallup (n.d.). State of the Global Workplace: 2023 Report. Gallup Workplace. https://www.gallup.com/workplace/349484/state-of-the-global-workplace.aspx
5. Sirdeshmukh, Deepak, Jagdip Singh, and Barry Sabol. "Consumer trust, value, and loyalty in relational exchanges." Journal of marketing 66, no. 1 (2002): 15-37.

1. THE TRUST GAP

1. Buckingham, Marcus. *First, Break All the Rules: What the World's Greatest Managers Do Differently*. New York, NY. :Simon & Schuster, 1999.
2. D. Sull, C. Sull, W. Cipolli, et al., "Why Every Leader Needs to Worry About Toxic Culture," MIT Sloan Management Review, March 16, 2022, https://sloanreview.mit.edu.

2. WHEN THE TRUST GAP GETS PERSONAL

1. Valles, Josue. "179 Words to Infuse Your Content with Emotion." LinkedID. https://www.linkedin.com/posts/josue-valles_want-to-make-your-content-more-memorable-activity-7092877805599797248-wmHa?utm_source=share&utm_medium=member_desktop.
2. "Developing and Sustaining Employee Engagement." SHRM. SHRM, https://www.shrm.org/resourcesandtools/tools-and-samples/toolkits/pages/sustainingemployeeengagement.aspx.

3. EPIDEMIC OF DISTRUST

1. "Definition of Epidemic." Merriam-Webster. Merriam-Webster, https://www.merriam-webster.com/dictionary/epidemic#:~:text=noun-,1,rapid%20spread%2C%20growth%2C%20or%20development.
2. Kennedy, Brian, Alec Tyson, and Cary Funk. "Americans' Trust in Scientists, Other Groups Declines." Pew Research Center, (2022): 1-25. https://www.pewresearch.org/science/wp-content/uploads/sites/16/2022/02/PS_2022.02.15_trust-declines_REPORT.pdf.
3. Kennedy, Brian, Alec Tyson, and Cary Funk. "Americans' Trust in Scientists, Other Groups Declines."
4. "Trust and Distrust in America." Pew Research Center. Pew Research Center, July 22, 2019.
5. "Trust and Distrust in America." Pew Research Center.
6. Iacurci, Greg. "2022 Was the 'Real Year of the Great Resignation,' Says Economist." CNBC. CNBC, February 1, 2023. https://www.cnbc.com/2023/02/01/why-2022-was-the-real-year-of-the-great-resignation.html.
7. Schwantes, Marcel. "6 Toxic Phrases That Should Never Come Out of a Leader's Mouth." Inc. Inc., June 12, 2018. https://www.inc.com/marcel-schwantes/6-toxic-phrases-that-should-never-come-out-of-a-leaders-mouth.html?utm_source=linkedin&utm_medium=social&utm_campaign=freeform&cid=sf01002.
8. "The Meaning Behind the Biohazard Symbol | Esco Lifesciences Group." Esco Lifesciences Group. September 3, 2021. Video, https://www.youtube.com/watch?v=SzepzXoKF9I.
9. Shroder, John. "Biological Aspects of Hazards, Risks, and Disasters." Science Direct. Science Direct, July 9, 2015. https://www.sciencedirect.com/topics/engineering/biohazards#:~:text=Biological%20hazards%2C%20also%20known%20as,that%20can%20affect%20human%20health.

4. THE POWER OF TRUST

1. Jaffe, Dennis. "The Essential Importance Of Trust: How To Build It Or Restore It." Forbes. Forbes, December 5, 2018. https://www.forbes.com/sites/dennisjaffe/2018/12/05/the-essential-importance-of-trust-how-to-build-it-or-restore-it/?sh=4997876364fe.
2. Covey, Stephen M. R. 2008. *The Speed of Trust*. London, England: Simon & Schuster.
3. Sahakian, Barbara, and Jamie Nicole LaBuzetta. *Bad Moves: How decision making goes wrong, and the ethics of smart drugs*. OUP Oxford, 2013.
4. Robinson, Bryan. "5 Pivotal Soft Skills Essential For Success In Today's Global Market." Forbes. Forbes, February 3, 2023. https://www.forbes.com/sites/bryanrobinson/2023/02/03/5-pivotal-soft-skills-essential-for-success-in-todays-global-market/?sh=7a27e2a50f08.
5. "Believe It: Why Trust May Be the New Driver of Enterprise Value." Deloitte - CFO Insights. Deloitte, February 1, 2012. https://www2.deloitte.com/us/en/pages/finance/articles/cfo-insights-why-trust-may-be-the-new-driver-of-enterprise-value.html.
6. Jubenville, Colby. "Why Frameworks Are Essential To Organizational Success — Especially Right Now." Forbes. Forbes, November 12, 2021. https://www.forbes.com/sites/forbescoachescouncil/2021/11/12/why-frameworks-are-essential-to-organizational-success---especially-right-now/?sh=2e98f5a13956.
7. Aguiar, Marcos, Matthew Williams, Wendi Backler, Jeff Kiderman, François Candelon, Russell Dubner, Tawfik Hammoud, Ryoji Kimura, and Sharon Marcil. "What AI Reveals About Trust in the World'S Largest Companies." BCG. BCG, May 20, 2022. https://www.bcg.com/publications/2022/trust-index-analyzing-companies-trustworthiness.

5. THE TRUST PROPOSITION

1. CFI Team. "What Is a Value Proposition." CFI. CFI, https://corporatefinanceinstitute.com/resources/management/value-proposition/.
2. Carroll, Brian. "Direct from the Source: What a Value Proposition Is, what It Isn'T and the 5 Questions It Must Answer." Marketing Experiments Powered by MECLABS. MECLABS, March 30, 2015. https://marketingexperiments.com/value-proposition/value-proposition-michael-lanning#:~:text=Michael%20Lanning%20invented%20the%20term,proposition%E2%80%9D%20back%20in%20the%2080s.
3. Sirdeshmukh, Deepak, Jagdip Singh, and Barry Sabol. "Consumer trust, value, and loyalty in relational exchanges." Journal of marketing 66, no. 1

(2002): 15-37.

4. "Definition of Trust." Merriam-Webster. Merriam-Webster, https://www.merriam-webster.com/dictionary/trust.
5. "Definition of Proposition." Oxford Learner's Dictionary, https://www.oxfordlearnersdictionaries.com/us/definition/american_english/proposition_1#:~:text=proposition-,noun,a%20business%20proposition%20to%20you.

6. THE STRUCTURE OF TRUST

1. Gupta, Shalene. "There's a Trust Gap between Business Leaders, Employees, and Consumers. This Is Why." Fast Company. Fast Company, March 28, 2023. https://www.fastcompany.com/90871322/pwc-study-business-companies-trust-gap.
2. Clear, James. *Atomic Habits: An easy & proven way to build good habits & break bad ones*. Penguin: Avery, 2018.
3. Sirdeshmukh, Deepak, Jagdip Singh, and Barry Sabol. "Consumer trust, value, and loyalty in relational exchanges." Journal of marketing 66, no. 1 (2002): 15-37.
4. "Organizational Competence in the Management and Support of Projects." Project Management Institute. Project Management Institute, September 7, 2000. https://www.pmi.org/learning/library/organizational-competence-management-support-projects-8600.
5. Reed, S. K. (2017). *Problem solving*. In S. E. F. Chipman (Ed.), The Oxford handbook of cognitive science (pp. 231–247). Oxford University Press.
6. "Your Best Culture Already Exists." Gallup. Gallup, https://www.gallup.com/workplace/229832/culture.aspx?utm_source=google&utm_medium=cpc&utm_campaign=workplace_non-branded_cuture&utm_term=corporate%20culture&utm_content=culture_audit&gclid=Cj0KCQjw9fqnBhDSARIsAHlcQYT2B08itdJ_nYlKwZLEmuaAbion6MkvCZDe9Jl17M2IeXbQhJhRHfQaAnFDEALw_wcB.
7. "Following Policies and Procedures, and why It'S Important." PowerDMS by NeoGov. NeoGov, December 18, 2020. https://www.powerdms.com/policy-learning-center/following-policies-and-procedures-and-why-its-important#:~:text=Policies%20and%20procedures%20keep%20operations,be%20quickly%20identified%20and%20addressed.

7. BUILDING BLOCK OF TRUST #1: COMPETENCY

1. Wikipedia. 2023. "Perfect Game (Baseball)." Wikimedia Foundation. Last modified September 16, 2023. https://en.wikipedia.org/wiki/Perfect_game_(baseball).
2. Simon, Andrew. "A Look at All 24 Perfect Games in AL/NL History." MLB. MLB.Com, June 28, 2023. https://www.mlb.com/news/all-time-perfect-games.
3. "Phillies Vs. Astros Pat Hoberg 2022-10-29." Ump Scorecards. Ump Scorecards, October 29, 2022. https://www.umpscorecards.com/single_game/?game_id=715723.
4. "What Are Competencies?" Office of Human Resources. National Institutes of Health, Accessed October 8, 2023. https://hr.nih.gov/about/faq/working-nih/competencies/what-are-competencies#:~:text=Competencies%20are%20the%20knowledge%2C%20skills,repeatedly%20applying%20knowledge%20or%20ability.
5. Prahalad, C.K., and Gary Hamel. "The Core Competence of the Corporation." Harvard Business Review https://www.scirp.org/(S(lz5mqp453ed-snp55rrgjct55.))/reference/referencespapers.aspx?referenceid=1881408.
6. Collins, Jim. 2001. *Good to Great*. London, England: Random House Business Books.
7. Collins, Jim. *Good to Great*.
8. George, Steve. "Competence and Competency Frameworks." CIPD. CIPD, https://www.cipd.org/en/knowledge/factsheets/competency-factsheet/#:~:text=The%20framework%20should%20contain%20definitions,competency%20%E2%80%93%20the%20behaviours%20deemed%20unacceptable.

8. BUILDING BLOCK OF TRUST #2: PROBLEM-SOLVING

1. Hobbs, Candler. "Working Out the Problems of Apollo 13." Georgia Tech College of Engineering. Georgia Tech, April 15, 2020. https://coe.gatech.edu/news/2020/04/working-out-problems-apollo-13.
2. Reed, S. K. (2017). Problem solving. In S. E. F. Chipman (Ed.), The Oxford handbook of cognitive science (pp. 231–247). Oxford University Press.
3. Hammond, John S., Ralph L. Keeney, and Howard Raiffa. "The Hidden Traps in Decision Making." Harvard Business Review. Harvard Business

Review, October 1, 1998. https://hbr.org/1998/09/the-hidden-traps-in-decision-making-2.
4. Hammond, John S., Ralph L. Keeney, and Howard Raiffa. "The Hidden Traps in Decision Making."
5. "What Is Appreciative Inquiry? A Short Guide to the Appreciative Inquiry Model & Process." Benedictine University. Benedictine University, May 9, 2017. https://cvdl.ben.edu/blog/what-is-appreciative-inquiry/.
6. "What Is Appreciative Inquiry? A Short Guide to the Appreciative Inquiry Model & Process." Benedictine University.

9. BUILDING BLOCK OF TRUST #3: CARE FOR OTHERS

1. Merriam-Webster. Merriam-Webster, https://www.merriam-webster.com/dictionary/benevolence.
2. Sirdeshmukh, Deepak, Jagdip Singh, and Barry Sabol. "Consumer trust, value, and loyalty in relational exchanges." Journal of marketing 66, no. 1 (2002): 15-37.
3. Mwenda, Mike. "Tim the Elephant Dies in Kenya: Africa Loses One of Its Last Giant Tuskers." Lifegate Daily. Lifegate, March 2, 2020. https://www.lifegate.com/tim-the-elephant-dies.
4. Mwenda, Mike. "Tim the Elephant Dies in Kenya: Africa Loses One of Its Last Giant Tuskers."
5. Mwenda, Mike. "Tim the Elephant Dies in Kenya: Africa Loses One of Its Last Giant Tuskers."
6. Harry Weger Jr. , Gina R. Castle & Melissa C. Emmett (2010) Active Listening in Peer Interviews: The Influence of Message Paraphrasing on Perceptions of Listening Skill, International Journal of Listening, 24:1, 34-49.
7. Abrahams, Robin, and Boris G. "How to Become a Better Listener." Harvard Business Review. Harvard Business Review, December 21, 2021. https://hbr.org/2021/12/how-to-become-a-better-listener.
8. Swinand, Andrew. "Why Kindness at Work Pays Off." Harvard Business Review. Harvard Business Review, July 21, 2023. https://hbr.org/2023/07/why-kindness-at-work-pays-off.

10. TRUSTWORTHY PEOPLE

1. Sinha, Ruchi. "New to the Team? Here'S How to Build Trust (Remotely)." Harvard Business Review. Harvard Business Review, March 23, 2021. https://hbr.org/2021/03/new-to-the-team-heres-how-to-build-trust-remotely.
2. Levesque, Elizabeth M. "Understanding the Skills Gap—And what Employers Can Do about It." Brookings. Brookings, December 6, 2019. https://www.brookings.edu/articles/understanding-the-skills-gap-and-what-employers-can-do-about-it/.
3. DeLizonna, Laura. "High-Performing Teams Need Psychological Safety: Here'S How to Create It." Harvard Business Review. Harvard Business Review, August 24, 2017. https://hbr.org/2017/08/high-performing-teams-need-psychological-safety-heres-how-to-create-it.
4. Godin, Seth. "The Warning Signs of Defending the Status Quo." Seth's Blog. August 29, 2011. https://seths.blog/2011/08/the-warning-signs-of-defending-the-status-quo/.
5. Petry, Carson. "Unchecked Ego: The Dangerous Impact of Those in Positions of Authority." LinkedIn. March 4, 2023. https://www.linkedin.com/pulse/unchecked-ego-dangerous-impact-those-positions-authority-carson-petry/.
6. DeLizonna, Laura. "High-Performing Teams Need Psychological Safety: Here'S How to Create It." Harvard Business Review. Harvard Business Review, August 24, 2017. https://hbr.org/2017/08/high-performing-teams-need-psychological-safety-heres-how-to-create-it.

11. TRUSTWORTHY POLICIES AND PRACTICES

1. Hemus, Jonathan. "How to Get the CEO Apology Right." LinkedIN. January 27, 2020. https://www.linkedin.com/pulse/how-get-ceo-apology-right-jonathan-hemus/.
2. Hemus, Jonathan. "How to Get the CEO Apology Right."
3. "Following Policies and Procedures, and why It's Important." PowerDMS. PowerDMS, December 18, 2020. https://www.powerdms.com/policy-learning-center/following-policies-and-procedures-and-why-its-important#:~:text=Policies%20and%20procedures%20are%20an,making%2C%20and%20streamline%20internal%20processes.
4. Cook, Brier. "Do You Know the Average Time Spent in Meetings?" Fellow. Fellow, February 28, 2023. https://fellow.app/blog/meetings/do-you-

know-the-average-time-spent-in-meetings/.

5. Lencioni, Patrick. 2004. Death by Meeting: A Leadership Fable...About Solving the Most Painful Problem in Business. Jossey-Bass. https://www.amazon.com/Death-Meeting-Leadership-Solving-Business/dp/0787968056.
6. Saunders, Elizabeth G. "Do You Really Need to Hold That Meeting?" Harvard Business Review. Harvard Business Review, March 20, 2015. https://hbr.org/2015/03/do-you-really-need-to-hold-that-meeting.
7. "The Pirates Gave a Season Ticket Holder a Foul Ball that Landed in Their Seat." SBNation. SBNation, August 11, 2020. https://www.sbnation.com/mlb/2020/8/11/21363250/pirates-season-ticket-holder-foul-ball-good-news.
8. "The Pirates Gave a Season Ticket Holder a Foul Ball that Landed in Their Seat." SBNation.

12. TAKING ACTION ON TRUST

1. Olson, Emily. "Giant Blobs of Seaweed Are Hitting Florida. That's when the Real Problem Begins." NPR. NRP, May 9, 2023. https://www.npr.org/2023/05/09/1174944656/giant-blobs-of-seaweed-are-hitting-florida-thats-when-the-real-problem-begins.
2. Sull, Donald, and Charles Sull. "How to Fix a Toxic Culture." MIT Sloan Management Review. MIT Sloan Management Review, September 28, 2022. https://sloanreview.mit.edu/article/how-to-fix-a-toxic-culture/.
3. Freedman, Joshua. "Three Key Strategies from Stephen MR Covey: How to Lead with Trust & Optimize Wellbeing." Six Seconds: The Emotional Intelligence Network. https://www.6seconds.org/2017/10/31/stephen-mr-covey-three-key-strategies/.
4. Freedman, Joshua. "Three Key Strategies from Stephen MR Covey: How to Lead with Trust & Optimize Wellbeing."
5. Sirdeshmukh, Deepak, Jagdip Singh, and Barry Sabol. "Consumer trust, value, and loyalty in relational exchanges." Journal of marketing 66, no. 1 (2002): 15-37.
6. Barnett, Paul. "If What Gets Measured Gets Managed, Measuring the Wrong Thing Matters." Thomson Reuters. February 1, 2015. https://static.store.tax.thomsonreuters.com/static/relatedresource/CMJ--15-01%20sample-article.pdf.

ACKNOWLEDGMENTS

In so many ways, this is not "my" book. This is "our" book. *Closing the Trust Gap* has the fingerprints of so many people on it, and I will always be grateful for the positive influence of those people. Writing this book alone would have been impossible.

A very special thank you to my wife, Jamie, and our four incredible children: Cailyn, Isaac, Evan, and Levi. Jamie has not only been my voice of encouragement, she has also been my voice of reason, supporting me with unconditional love. The very title of this book, *Closing the Trust Gap*, was first suggested by Jamie while we were driving west on I-70 towards Colorado. Simply put, this book would not be in existence without her. In so many ways, she is the co-author of this book, because she daily lives out what it means to be trustworthy. And to my wonderful children: I'm so proud of you, and I'm so grateful to be your father.

Thank you Kurt Bartolich, Founder and CEO of BrandCertain. Kurt's approach to helping organizations reposition their brands through quantitative research is brilliant, and I've learned so much from his relentless commitment to sound data that is both practical and actionable. I can't thank you enough for inviting me into co-authoring the *National Survey on Brand*

and Trust with you. During one of my many conversations with Kurt, who is an outstanding author in his own right, Kurt challenged me with the question, "Why haven't you written a book?" My internal dialogue was rattling through the excuses: Fear of failure? Insecurity? Fractured priorities? Apathy? Imposter Syndrome? Lack of clarity? Perceived lack of time? Kurt's pointed question became fuel for me to endure through competing priorities, unexpected life interruptions, and the very real challenges of distilling seemingly disparate thoughts into a book. Thank you, Kurt.

Thank you Justin Ricklefs, the owner of a soulful and sophisticated human-first marketing agency called Guild Collective. Justin challenged me several years ago in a way that was uncomfortable, unsettling and necessary. I was waffling back and forth on whether to build upon my doctoral work and deepen my ongoing interest in starting a company focused on helping leaders, teams, and organizations strengthen trust. Justin said: "If you don't share this work about trust with the world, you are being selfish, and you are not stewarding what you have been gifted." It was a critical moment for me because Justin, who I trust implicitly, spoke truth to me and called me to action.

I also want to thank the entire team at Streamline Books. A cup of coffee with Will Severns, co-founder of Streamline Books, at Thou Mayest in downtown Kansas City has led to this. I will always be grateful, Will…the next cup of coffee is on me. Thank you to my developmental editor, Jennifer Glover. Your wisdom, insight, and support throughout this process has been remarkable. You pushed me to find and write with a new voice, and I can't thank you enough. For my project manager, Christen Carlson: thank you for keeping me on track. Without you, I may still be on chapter 2! Thank you to my Copy Editor, Andrew Blackburn. Your attention to detail is amazing. You care deeply for every punctuation mark and every letter! Thank you to Hannah Crabb for capturing the essence of the book in the design of the cover. Thank you to Director of Operations, Trevor Waite, for moving this book from a document to published!

Thank you to the following people who have been instrumental in this process:

To my brother Darin (and Heather) and my sister Stacey (and John). You are the best, and I'm so grateful for frequent group text messages and holiday gatherings filled with laughter. Thank you to the rest of my family for your unending support.

There are so many other people to thank for their encouragement throughout this book writing journey: Chip Huber, John Newsom, Ethan Beute, Chris Stathos, Marcus Mossberger, Brad Hill, Richard Manley-Tannis, Blake Shaw, Brad Garstang, Kelli Schutte, Trey Griggs, Matt Hemingway, Ivan Pancic, Paul Price, Merle Mees, Caleb Eissler, Chris Stathos, Rob and Kami Williams, Micah Salazar, Kelly Broadway, Mark McAuliffe, Erica Schmitz-Morgan, Leslie Qullico, André Davis, Maki Moussavi, Katie Ervin, Jenna Scott, Andy Pitts, Jay Minnick, Frank Armato, Sandy Stover, Aaron Lawrence and Brett Jackson at Intrepid Creative, David Byrd, Todd Hagemann, Racheal Burnett, Jeremy Parson, Jason Muir, Jeremy Tucker, and many others.

Thank you to my father, Stan Scheer, whose memory is still very much alive for all who knew him. He lived out trust in ways seen, unseen, known, and unknown. I thought about him many times as I was writing this book, and I'm so grateful for his ongoing legacy. I love you, Dad.

Finally, thank you to the reader. Thank you for prioritizing the vital topic of trust. Thank you for taking action on trust and for your commitment to closing the trust gap.

ABOUT TRUSTCENTRIC™

TrustCentric™ Consulting is an organizational and leadership development firm that helps organizations succeed by developing trusted people and trusted practices.

TrustCentric™ helps leaders, teams, and organizations keep trust at the center of everything they do by defining reality with reliable data, implementing a proven trust-building framework, and walking alongside clients to develop clear, obtainable, accountable, long-lasting, and trustworthy strategies for success.

Core solutions that TrustCentric™ provides include:

- In-depth TrustCentric Organizational Trust Assessments©
- Executive Leader Coaching
- Team Coaching
- Structure of Trust™ Cohorts (online / in person) for individuals or teams
- Strengthening Organizational Trust Retreats
- Strategic Plan Development
- Various Organizational and Leadership Development Workshops

- Six-Month Frontline Organizational Leadership Development Programs
- Keynote / Seminar Speaking
- Focus Group Facilitation
- Online Course: The Complete Guide to Building Organizational Trust
- Ongoing Organizational and Leadership Development Support through retainer and fractional support engagements

Every organizational and leadership solution TrustCentric™ provides starts with trust.

To learn more about how TrustCentric™ could provide support for you, your team, or your organization:

Web: www.TrustCentricConsulting.com
Email: cory@TrustCentricConsulting.com

For resources and reflection questions to help guide discussions with your team or organization, go to:

www.TrustCentricConsulting.com/Resources

ABOUT THE AUTHOR

Cory Scheer is the Founder and CEO of TrustCentric™ Consulting, an organizational and leadership development firm. In addition to over twenty-five years in leadership roles in multiple sectors, Cory has obtained an Executive MBA (Rockhurst University) and a Doctorate in Educational Leadership and Policy Analysis (University of Missouri). Cory has worked with small businesses, school districts, corporations, nonprofit organizations, higher education institutions, ministries, the military, and municipalities to provide vital support and clear direction on how to ensure people, practices, and policies become more trustworthy so that key performance indicators improve. Cory and his wife live in Kansas City, Missouri with their 4 children.

ABOUT THE AUTHOR